What the experts are saying about David Toma . . .

"There is no one like David Toma. . . . His forty years of experience and his intense love and commitment have changed millions of young lives."

—BARRY SMITH, M.D., PH.D., director of the Health Foundation

"David Toma is a giant among giants—there has never been, nor ever will be, someone with his expertise and with such limitless concern for every teenager he meets. His remarkable gift for reaching out to the kids' very souls—where no one else has been able to reach—has saved millions of lives."

—JOSEPH MAUDI, M.D., director of Union Memorial Hospital's Drug and Alcohol Treatment Center

What teenagers are saying about David Toma . . .

"He's fantastic, he's excellent. For the first time somebody really cared about me when I needed help."

—a junior from Monroe, Michigan

"Listening to him is like listening to my life story."

—a freshman from Pennsauken, New Jersey

"He doesn't talk like someone who is just preaching. He tells it from experience."

—a senior from Detroit, Michigan

"I think he hits home with a lot of people. He shows what drugs can do, the effect it can have on you. A lot of kids don't know."

—a junior from San Diego, California

"I think he is great because he talks about real-life stuff. It's not made up. He's lived through it."

—a senior from Auburn, New York

"Toma made me proud not to be on drugs. I know people in my class who experiment with drugs and alcohol and I hope adults realize that kids need someone around to talk to."

—a sixth grader from Marlborough, Connecticut

Turning Your Life Around

David Toma's Guide for Teenagers

DAVID TOMA
and Christopher Biffle

HarperPerennial

A Division of HarperCollins*Publishers*

HarperCollins books may be purchased for educational, business, or sales promotional use. For information, please call or write: Special Markets Department, HarperCollins Publishers, Inc., 10 East 53rd Street, New York, NY 10022. Telephone: (212) 207-7528; Fax: (212) 207-7222.

FIRST EDITION

Designed by Cassandra J. Pappas

Library of Congress Cataloging-in-Publication Data
Toma, David.
    Turning your life around: David Toma's guide for teenagers/David Toma and Christopher Biffle. —1st ed.
        p.   cm.
    ISBN 0-06-096830-3
    1. Teenagers—Conduct of life. 2. Teenagers—Religious life. I. Biffle, Christopher. II. Title.
BJ1661.T59   1992
646.7'00835—dc20   91-55469

92 93 94 95 96 DT/RRD 10 9 8 7 6 5 4 3 2 1

To all the kids of the world
who have touched my life,
this is for you.
I love you all.

—DAVID TOMA

To the memory of
Genevieve Oliva
whose life was
dedicated to love.

—CHRISTOPHER BIFFLE

Contents

PART 1: GETTING STARTED

PART 2: SEVEN BIG PROBLEMS

PART 3: YOU AND GOD

Acknowledgments

This book is based on almost forty years of lecturing and listening to millions of kids and parents, and some of the many questions that have been asked of me. I couldn't use all of the questions because they are too numerous, but have used the ones that have come up most often. I could not have written this book without the many people that I have relied on from time to time for information, guidance, inspiration, and, most of all, my sanity: Dr. Seymour Wexler, a good friend and confidant as well as mentor, and someone who really cares about people; Dr. Frank Spirn, an inspiration as well as educator; Dr. Roger Brodkin, a good friend and communicator; Dr. Richard Boiardo, who, when I needed him, was always there; Dr. Peter Kelly, who took much of his time to listen and to evaluate situations with me; Dr. Jerry Grubman, who educated me on venereal diseases and AIDS; Dr. Joseph Prestifillippo, an oral surgeon who kept me informed on what tobacco and snuff do to the mouth and throat and oral cancer; Dr. James McGuire; Joseph T. Stowasky and Gene Schafhauser, registered pharmacists who contributed some of the information I needed to know about drugs and their side effects.

A special thanks to Jack Dreyfus for his ongoing commitment, and true dedication to helping people all over the world. I love you.

My thanks to Detective Joseph Pariso, who I worked with for

so many years on the streets of Newark, New Jersey, who became one of the leading authorities on drugs and alcohol, and who, from time to time, has kept me up to date on the kind of street knowledge that American kids can relate to.

I want to especially thank my agent, Al Zuckerman, and my cowriter, Chris Biffle, for believing in me and realizing how important this book is for *all* people.

This book would never have been put together in its proper form without the patience, expertise, and knowledge of my assistant editor at HarperCollins, Peternelle van Arsdale.

Most importantly, I must thank the thousands upon thousands of psychologists, psychiatrists, mental health workers, doctors, school principals, superintendents, teachers, and nurses who worked with all the kids and parents during and after my speeches. They were always there to help the kids in crisis, and were a big factor in my reaching out and touching lives. I am gratefully indebted to the parents and organizations who worked so hard to get me to their towns, cities, and states.

Perhaps my greatest debt of all is to my wife, Pat, who had the patience and understanding to put up with my many moods after criss-crossing America each and every week, and hearing story after story of so many kids in trouble. Also, my children, James, Patricia Ann, Donna, and Janice—as well as my five grandchildren, Kellie, David, Jesse, David, and Jenna. Just looking at them inspired me to go on for their sake.

Finally, I must thank all of the kids (too numerous to count) who over the years would constantly say, "Please don't stop doing what you're doing." They made it all worthwhile. I needed them and I love them all. Through all of the years of traveling, it became lonely and depressing most of the time, but I always had my friend to keep me company and give me the will to go on—so I say thank you God.

To Toni and Al—Thanks!

For all your love, only we understand.

—*David Toma*

Making This Book Work for You

by Louis A. Tartaglia, M.D.

Louis A. Tartaglia, M.D., is a psychiatrist, medical director of the Alliance for Recovery, and medical coordinator of the Mother Teresa Institute of Recovery in Rome, Italy.

You may not understand what you have in your hands as you open this book to begin working on yourself. Or you may be giving this book as a gift to a troubled teenager whom you would like to help. This book is an extremely powerful tool that can help open up even the most closed down, resistant teenager. This is what David Toma does best. He can reach inside and connect with even the most defensive kids. I've watched Toma work as I have sat in on some of his personal counseling sessions. He connects with the pain kids feel, and they trust him. How he does it is not nearly as important as the fact that he does it consistently with hundreds of thousands of the toughest kids to reach. Finally, he and Christopher Biffle have put together a book that is so much like being with David that it can be used by anyone to help reach out to someone in trouble.

In using this book, or giving it to someone else, you should be aware that it could open up some painful wounds that will need to be healed. There is a resources section in the back of this book that includes telephone numbers of organizations that can help you—I encourage you to use them. If you're giving this book to someone else, please also make yourself available to talk one on one. You may need to call some of the help numbers yourself or find a good counselor if necessary.

Turning Your Life Around is a chance for teenagers and the adults who care about them to experience David's uncanny ability to ask—and answer—questions and to identify what is really going on inside. For the counselors who plan to use this book as an aid to therapy or counseling, I congratulate you on your "street smarts." You will be amazed at how quickly your clients will open up with David.

And finally, to the kid who is still out there using drugs or alcohol, or in pain over how tough life has been for you, I'd like to introduce you to a friend of mine. His name is David Toma. He is unlike any other individual I have ever met. He'll listen to you. Take him home with you and have a heart-to-heart talk. You can tell him anything, he has heard it all. He understands.

Part 1

Getting Started

Your life may be extremely difficult right now. You may feel very depressed or even hopeless. Drug or alcohol addiction, involvement with Satanism, or serious family problems might be leading you to seriously think about suicide. If this is true, put this book down and call 1-800-882-3386. This is the number of the Suicide Prevention Hotline. These people are extremely competent professionals and will give you all the help you need. The call is toll-free. Please, don't wait another minute.

1

Introduction

If you're a teenager and you're depressed about school or your relationships with your family, friends, or someone you love; if you have a drug or alcohol problem; or if you're simply tired of the way your life is going, then this book is not just for you, *it's about you*.

My name is David Toma and you might think I don't know anything about your life. I get five thousand letters **a week** from teenagers. Every year I talk to more than **one and a half million** students in schools all over the country. And I've been doing this for forty years! I'm not bragging, but I've probably helped more young people solve their problems than anyone alive.

This book is a conversation between you and me based on insights I've gained helping countless teenagers understand themselves. I'm going to help you tell your story so that you can see your world more clearly. Along the way, I'll tell you stories teenagers have told me so that you can learn about your life by comparing it to others. When I think you need it, I'll give you some advice so that in the future you can act with knowledge not ignorance. But the real healing in this book will not come from me but you. In every chapter you'll be adding the information that will turn this book into the story of your new life. You're the world's greatest expert on your world, your relationships, and your problems. I'm going to help you teach yourself what you need to know.

First we'll talk about your relationships and your past, so you can see what's led you to where you are today. We'll discuss your mother, your father, your friends, and the worst times in your life and the best. Little by little, you'll see your life more clearly than you ever have before. You'll understand your relationship with your parents and your friends, you'll see why you do the things you do when you're in love, you'll learn what weakens your new life, and what gives it strength. You'll see what is wonderful in your life, what is worth fighting for, and what must be left behind.

In the second part of our conversation, we'll talk about some of the most serious problems teenagers face. Self-hatred, destructive anger at others, depression, suicidal feelings, drugs, alcohol, involvement in Satanism. No scientist, sociologist, psychologist, or reporter has talked to even 1 percent of the young people I have in the last forty years. I have heard enough horror stories to fill an encyclopedia. I'm going to share the experiences of other teenagers with you in order to help you understand your own problems more deeply than you ever thought possible. I'm going to tell you some things you've never heard or even dreamed. I'm not trying to scare you. I just want you to know the truth. When you finish this section you'll have powerful, new insights about the causes of your pain. Carefully work through each chapter that applies to you; read the others for the information they contain.

In the last part of our conversation, we'll talk about God. I've **never** known a teenager who has solved serious personal problems without a relationship with God or, as some prefer to say, "a higher power." In the final section of this book, you will decide if you're ready to seek God's help. If you are, I'll help you to see your spiritual life more clearly and give you some ideas that will strengthen your relationship with Him. Then you'll be ready to start doing something amazing. We'll work together on a one-week plan to help you start living the first chapter of your new life.

The path ahead is not going to be easy, but you've already taken the first step. You probably have friends who would never be doing what you're doing right now . . . reading a book about finding a new life. But before you pat yourself on the back, listen to me, **don't think just reading the words in this book will magically change you.** I know the path, but you're the one who has to walk it. I know my methods work, but it's up to you whether or not you're ready for them. Since 1951 in every state in our nation, I've helped tens of thousands of teenagers make remarkable changes in their lives. Teenage alcoholics, drug abusers, prostitutes, gang bangers, all kinds of troubled teens have used my techniques to become new people. But every kid I've helped had one thing in common, he or she had the guts to fight for a new life.

If you've even picked up this book, then you're thinking about a new beginning. You're tired of how you've lived. You're ready to find something better.

Make your decision now. Are you ready to start your new life?

Dave, _____

_____.

Turn to chapter 2 if you're ready to begin.

2

You and Me

As I said, this book is a conversation between you and me.

Let's start by introducing ourselves. As you already know, my name's Dave Toma. I've had an amazing life.

I was a cop for twenty-one years, and for sixteen of those years I was a detective in the vice, gambling, and narcotic squad of one of the most troubled cities in the world: Newark, New Jersey. Nobody ever had an arrest record like mine. I arrested thousands and had a 98 percent conviction rate. A 25 percent conviction rate is enough in most places to get you a reputation as a great cop.

I specialized in fighting the Mafia, the mob, and the underworld. I've been shot, stabbed, and put in the hospital more than thirty times. Despite all this, I never had to use my gun. I used my wits and disguises to catch crooks. I'd ride around town with my disguises laid out on the backseat of the car. If a guy began to catch on that I was following him, I would pull into an alley and in two minutes I could make myself up as a priest or a bum or even sometimes as a woman. I must have been good. I had guys proposition me and, believe me, I made an ugly woman.

As a cop, I was throwing people in jail right and left. The other cops were jealous, but I didn't care. I felt like I was cleaning up Newark single-handed. But the whole time I was frustrated. I was great at getting people put away, but it drove me crazy that I couldn't help them. My captain used to say, "Don't worry about it,

Toma. They're just scum. Lock 'em up and forget 'em." But I couldn't do that. I remember this one skinny little kid, Danny, a heroin addict. He was about nineteen and I'd been picking him up since he was thirteen. I must have busted this kid ten times. One night I found him lying behind a Dumpster outside a bar. He was just lying there on his side in the garbage, eyes closed. I didn't know if he was dead or passed out. I leaned over and felt his pulse on his neck. I had a hard time finding it. I was just about to head back for my squad car to call an ambulance when he came to. He said something to me that I'll never forget: *"Dave, don't arrest me. Help me."*

Everyone called me a tough cop but it was all I could do to keep from crying.

Even though I wasn't supposed to, I rode to the hospital in the ambulance with the poor kid in my arms. He could barely talk. He whispered he was hooked so bad he needed two hundred bucks a day and he could only make that kind of money by turning tricks. He wore shirts with long sleeves so the Johns wouldn't see the purple bruises from the needle all over his arms. The next day, I went looking for his mother. The neighbors said she'd been on a heroin jag for a week and nobody knew where she was. I'm glad I didn't find her.

I went home and I was so mad, I wanted to kick in the walls. But here's the truth. It took a lot of Dannys before I got the message. The cop who was so great at throwing people in jail was part of the problem. The people I arrested needed my help, and all I was doing was putting them behind bars. I decided that maybe I could help by going around to schools to talk to kids about drugs. It was easier for me to face a guy with a gun than it was for me to face an auditorium full of teenagers who thought they knew it all. I told them about the lives I saw ruined by drugs and alcohol. I wasn't very good at it at first. I was just another adult preaching at them. But before long, I found ways of communicating. I talked to kids in a language they understood. I told it straight. I didn't pull any punches and I didn't take crap from the smart guys in the audience. I told them I wasn't their baby-sitter. I told them I'd fought the Mafia for years and put guys in jail who would have had them for breakfast. I invited the smart guys to come down front and see how tough they were. Nobody ever took me up on it.

I talked to thousands of kids and I could tell I was getting through to them, but it wasn't enough. I had to take my message nationwide. It was a tough battle, but I convinced Hollywood I had a great story. I'm the only person in the world who has had two television series based on his life, "Toma" and "Baretta." These series gave me plenty of publicity, and I used it all to take my message about drugs and alcohol to teenagers all across the country. Publishers asked me to write a book. I wrote four. Each one was a best-seller. I used the publicity from my books to get bigger audiences to listen to my message. My message is this: The lives of teenagers are being ruined by drugs, alcohol, and a host of other problems too strong for anyone to cope with alone.

I started my career by focusing on drugs and alcohol, but the millions of kids I've talked to have changed me. I've heard countless stories of lives nearly ruined by divorce, child abuse, venereal disease, Satanism . . . you name it. I thought I would have to write a book to help teens deal with every one of these topics, and maybe I will someday, but I realized recently that the *result of every problem teenagers face is always the same*. Teenagers don't know what to do with their lives. Their old lives are so devastating that they can see no way into the future. No matter what their problem is, kids ask me one question over and over again, "Dave, what am I going to do?"

Listen to me. This book is going to give you the insight and information you need to start a new life. I've learned no single answer is right for everyone. That's why this book is going to be about **your** mother, **your** father, **your** feelings, **you. This book is like no other on earth. It is the story of your victory over your old life and your journey toward the future.**

I figure in my life I've talked to over thirty million teenagers about their problems in lectures, and there is no way of counting how many people of all ages I've reached on television and radio. But none of that matters now. Right now, I'm talking to just you.

Tell me about yourself.

You stop and think for a few minutes and then you say:

Dave, I'm the kind of person who _____

_____.

When you first see me you might think _____

_____

_____.

As you get to know me you'd find out _____

_____

_____.

The best things about me are _____

_____.

The worst things about me are _____

_____.

The reason I picked up this book is _____

_____

_____.

What I want for my future is _____

_____.

That's a beginning. Now, let's take one more step.

3

Opening Up

One of the best ways I've found to help teenagers is to get them to open up and talk. The great thing about this book is that it's just between you and me. Say anything you want. If you're mad, be mad. If you hurt, go ahead and let yourself hurt. If you want to cuss out your parents or your teachers, go ahead. Maybe you've got something that is eating you up inside. Get it out. Before we go any further, just tell me what is bothering you the most.

As you think about what you want to say, inside you feel ____

_____

_____

_____.

You are thinking about _____

_____

_____

_____.

And then you say:

Okay, Dave. I'm going to try opening up. I've got to say that what is bothering me most in my life right now is _____

_____

_____

_____

_____.

This bothers me so much because _____

_____

_____

_____.

I feel _____

_____

_____.

To help you explore your feelings more, I'm going to tell you about some conversations I've had with teenagers recently. You may feel like you have a terrible home life or only that you can't communicate with your parents as well as you would like. Maybe you've felt like killing yourself or maybe you're just aggravated at your teachers. It's been my experience that no matter the problem, if it is bothering you it's important. The conversations I'm going to relate to you are about both the worst and the best experiences of teenagers. I know you can learn something from each one.

I remember a red-haired girl who came up to me in Fontana, California, after one of my lectures. She had freckles like somebody had painted them all over her face. She said, "Mr. Toma, I've got to talk to somebody. My mom's an alcoholic and practically every weekend she's with a different guy. She makes me sick. She's lost about five jobs, and all she cares about is drinking. But here is the worst part. I think I'm starting to be just like her. Every weekend I go drinking with my friends. I hate it when my mom gets drunk but now I'm doing the same things! I've passed out and woke up in places and didn't know how I got there. I don't care about myself or what happens to me and I see that in her. It's so stupid but I can't help it. I drink because I'm angry at her for drinking. It's like I'm trying to get back at her for destroying herself so I try to destroy myself. I don't even hide it from her anymore. I want her to see what she is doing to me but she doesn't care, I guess, and that makes me not care either."

I asked her how old she was. She said the next day would be her fourteenth birthday. I told her, as I will tell you many times in our conversation, "You need to find someone to confide in. Find an older family member or a teacher, counselor, cop, nurse, doctor, Alcoholics Anonymous, *someone*. The worst thing you can do, absolutely the worst thing, is to keep your feelings to yourself. You have to get your pain out, you have to stop going round and round in circles inside your head. **You cannot solve your problems alone.**" I went on to say, "When you talk to someone else you will see your mother is sick. You have to be determined to not end up like her and never do to your kids what she has done to you. Never forget that if something happens to you while you're drinking, whether it be jail, hospital, pregnancy, or long-term mental damage, you are the one who is going to pay the price, not your mother. Take care of you. You are the most important person."

Is there any way you can relate to this girl's story? When you look at either of your parents, are you afraid that you have some of their worst characteristics?

Dave, the truth is _____

_____

_____.

When I look at my father, I see a man who _____

_____

_____.

Then when I look at myself, I see someone who _____

_____

_____

_____.

When I look at my mother, I see someone who _____

_____

_____

_____ .

Then when I look at myself, I see someone who _____

_____

_____

_____ .

When I think about all this, I realize _____

_____

_____ .

Here's another story to think about.

I recently met with six kids in upper New York State. Just talking to them a little, I could tell they had to be some of the most popular kids in the school. Two were cheerleaders, one boy had an academic scholarship to Duke, and a girl had a swimming scholarship to Notre Dame. They all were bright, well dressed, good looking. They'd reached me because after a party one night, they had all been talking and had discovered that each one of them was thinking about suicide. Two of the boys had even sat against a tree out in the woods and written their suicide notes. One of the boys, a blond-haired kid who had a scholarship to NYU, had brought his father's pistol but the other one chickened out and so he did too. I can see this blond kid so clearly. He was a little guy, about five foot four, 130 pounds, quiet voice, very serious.

"Dave," he said, "I don't know what's wrong with me. I feel empty. I've taken a lot of drugs, cocaine mostly, and that helped at first but I just feel sick, almost dead inside. I don't want to get any older. I don't want to grow up. Life sucks. It's like everything is dark inside and out. My parents are okay but I can't talk to them. I'm so sick of feeling rotten I just want to blow my brains out."

Some of the other kids nodded their heads. Each one had a different story to tell. One girl had been molested by her stepfather.

Another girl lived with her grandmother, and the grandmother had been in and out of psychiatric care. A boy had lost his father in a car crash and couldn't get over it. Every kid in the room had a drug habit and every one of those bright, good-looking kids, none over seventeen, was ready to end his or her life.

I said to them, "Think about what you're telling me. You are all into drugs and all of you are thinking about suicide. Doesn't that tell you something about the drugs you're doing? I know all of you have problems at home but those problems become compounded with the drugs. You begin to blame everyone for what you are going through. Each and every one of us in the world has a problem that always seems much worse than anyone else's, and if everyone thought like you kids, the whole world would commit suicide! Stop feeling sorry for yourselves. Quit the damn drugs and go out now and find someone to talk to. There are people out there who love you. Give them a chance. Open the door to your heart and let them in. It's amazing what a turnaround you will make. Remember suicide is final. There is no turning back. Call someone immediately when you get those feelings. You can't change your family situation unless you change your own life first. **The drugs must go now.**"

Now think about this conversation. Is there anything that rings a bell with you?

Dave, the worst I ever feel is when _____

_____

_____.

When I feel like that usually what I do is _____

_____

_____.

When I think about that now, I see _____

_____

_____.

We're going to come back to the problem of suicide and hit it hard, but for now, let me tell you a different kind of story. Last year I was in Florida and I met a kid I'll call Lenny. He's a short powerhouse with a chest like a beer barrel. He came bouncing up to me after one of my lectures saying, "Dave! Dave! Remember me?" I tried to but I couldn't. "I heard you when you were in Indianapolis, and I was the kid in the back of the auditorium who kept cracking jokes and you told me to get the hell out. Remember?" Then it came back to me. But man, had he changed! When I'd first seen him he was a long-haired, heavy-metal freak with a safety pin hanging from his ear. He had a foul mouth and he talked like he was the smartest, toughest kid in the world. We'd argued back and forth in the auditorium, and I'd finally told him what I thought of punks like him. He kicked over a few chairs and stormed out.

"Dave, you'll never believe this but you changed my life. I was acting like I was bad that day but inside I was scared. Everything felt out of control. I had a crack habit like you wouldn't believe. I was getting high before school, at lunch, and after school, man, forget it. In the month before you came, I'd wrecked three cars. My best friend had died from an overdose, and sometimes I couldn't stop crying about it. Even though crack had killed him, I was still using. Something about you got to me. I left but I still could hear you in my head. It was weird, it was like you were haunting me, telling me all the stuff I didn't want to hear but knew was right. The hardest thing I ever did was quit using. But I did. My family moved down to Florida and I been clean for six months." I told him I loved him more than he could know and then he hugged me and practically cracked my ribs!

Tell me what it would be like if you were free of the problems that plague you. Imagine your new life.

You think for a while about what your new life would be like. You see yourself happier, stronger, more in control. You see yourself leaving your old life behind. You say:

Dave, I can see _____

_____

_____

_____.

Thinking about that I feel _____

_____

_____.

The best thing I could do with my future would be _____

_____

_____.

"But how am I going to get there?"

Keep talking to me. You're already on the way.

4

Your Father

One good thing about this book is that you can change any part you want to. In this chapter we're going to talk about fathers and in the next, we're going to talk about mothers. If you want to change the subject from fathers and mothers to stepfathers or stepmothers or male or female guardians or your grandmother or grandfather, go ahead. Just think of these two chapters as helping you understand your relationship with the two most influential adults in your life.

If you ever heard me lecture, you know I don't talk very long before I start talking about my parents. My dad was an Italian immigrant who ruled our family with strength and love. He worked like a dog all his life, but he never complained. If he could put food on the table and help my mother he was happy. My mother had a terrible problem with her legs, they would swell up and be so painful she could hardly walk; she eventually died of this crippling arthritis. I can see my dad jumping up from the table, helping her across the kitchen, practically carrying her into the bedroom. He'd lift her legs up onto the bed, then rub them for hours and comfort her. He was the kind of man who was totally devoted to his wife. But he could be tough when he had to! I remember when he was old, about ninety-one, and all the kids were grown, he had us all over one day and made us sit down at the dinner table. Then he started in on us, "You! I hear you ain't talking to your sister! What kind of family is that? And you, you're not treating your wife like you should! How can you call yourself a man? And you, what the hell are you doing staying out late at night when you should be home with your children!" He kept going, ripping into us, and we were all afraid to say anything. Just with a few words, a look, he could turn us all into kids again. He had a power inside him that made us respect him.

Now, tell me a little about your dad. Is he similar to or different from my father?

Dave, my dad is the kind of man who _____

_____

_____.

I remember once when _____

_____

_____.

Another time _____

_____

_____.

My dad's best characteristics are _____

_____

_____.

My dad's worst characteristics are _____

_____

_____.

When I think about our relationship I feel _____

_____

_____,

because _____

_____.

Tell me more.

   On the outside my dad seems _____

_____

_____.

   Inside, he is a man who _____

_____

_____.

   His goal in life is to _____

_____.

   My strongest feelings about him are _____

_____

_____.

   The teenagers I talk to tell me everything. Here's a few fathers
that I've heard about. Maybe these stories will help you see your
dad more clearly.

   I remember once when I was up in Minneapolis talking to
teenagers in a rehab center, I asked them to tell me about their
parents. A tall, nervous boy with a brown pony tail raised his hand
and asked, "Dave, can I talk?" I said sure, go ahead.

   His lips were quivering and he had a hard time getting it out
but here is part of what he said. "My dad's in the Marines and I
used to think that was pretty neat. I had all this Marine Corps stuff
on the walls of my bedroom and whenever he'd come home, I'd
practically go crazy I was so happy. Sometimes he'd be gone for
months, sometimes only a week, but he was my hero. When he
came home I didn't want to do anything but be with him. Then one
night when I was about seven he came into my bedroom and started
talking about how he and my mom weren't getting along. I could

tell he had been drinking, but I felt great that he was confiding in me. It was like I was his buddy. After we had been talking a while he told me to stand up and take off my clothes so he could see what kind of man I was growing up to be. So I jumped up and took off my clothes and then he told me to walk over to the window and then come back. That seemed kind of strange but he was my dad, my hero. If he would have told me to jump out the window I probably would have. Then he told me that he didn't want to sleep with mom that night, could he get under the covers with me? Sure, I said. It was so neat to have my own dad sleeping in my bed. Then he took off his clothes and we got into bed together and then he started doing things to me. I didn't know what he was doing but I knew it was wrong. After that whenever he had been drinking and he and my mom were fighting he'd come into the bedroom. He kept going further and it was terrible. But there wasn't anybody I could turn to. He molested me for five years. Almost every time he came home it was the same thing. He'd start drinking, fighting with mom, and then I'd know what was going to happen and I couldn't do anything about it. If I met him now, I'd try to kill him."

There are many kinds of sexual abuse. They range from rape to fondling to sexually inappropriate "cuddling." Sexual abuse of children has reached epidemic proportions. Some teenagers, unlike this boy, don't realize that they have been abused as children. If you believe you need someone to talk to about a sexually abusive incident in your childhood, then don't put it off any longer. Find a counselor, teacher, minister, social worker, any adult you can trust and let him or her help you. Or call one of the numbers in the reference section on page 209. If you or your brothers or sisters have been threatened and told to keep quiet about what is happening at home, then it is especially important that you find someone to protect you. Call the police. Get whoever is harming you put into jail.

Maybe your father didn't physically abuse you, maybe his abuse was emotional. Or maybe he just ignored you. Let me tell you two brief stories and then I'll help you see your whole relationship with your dad more clearly. I remember a girl in Philadelphia, who was about sixty pounds overweight, told me that her father was nuts about her younger brother and Little League. She said, "This is going to sound strange but I think the reason I'm fat is because of my little brother. He's a nice kid, I love him, but as long as I can remember I've been jealous of him. He and my dad do everything together. I mean everything. They don't even eat with the family at the table. They go into the den and watch ESPN together, usually baseball. I remember once I broke my leg and my dad didn't come to the hospital for two days because he was helping my brother get ready for the playoffs! I can't remember my dad ever hugging me. I know on Christmas and for my birthdays, my mom always buys my presents. He makes it like a big joke. 'Let's see what I got you this year,' he says. So I think that's why I eat. I eat because I'm mad at him. I eat just to show him and everybody else I don't care."

I remember asking her, "Did overeating solve anything? Your dad has his priorities mixed up. He needs to be taught that each and every one of his kids is equal. They all need his love, attention, and respect. And if you don't get that from him then tell him or tell your mother or a counselor, tell someone. If you can't do this then write your dad a letter and leave it in his room. Sometimes a letter is more powerful than a conversation. If you just talk to him, then he can shut you off, but a letter gets to his heart and mind. Remember. Don't overeat or become anorexic or bulimic because of your dad or anyone. No one is worth it. You are too important, you have to respect and love yourself—even when you think no one else does."

Is there anything in this girl's relationship with her father that reminds you of your own relationship with your father?

I would have to say _____

_____

_____

_____

_____

_____.

Maybe this story will remind you of some of the positive things about your father.

Back when I was a cop I met a Sioux Indian who was crippled and trying to raise two girls by himself in one of the worst neighborhoods in Newark. His wife had died from tuberculosis, and when I knew him, his daughters were seven and nine. Whenever I saw them they were always together. They went to church together, they went to the park together, they went shopping together. He'd lost a leg in Korea, but he was very proud of how he could keep up with his kids, even on the playground. His only problem was he was too proud to accept welfare. I'll never forget one winter morning, it was just above zero, and I found him out on the street corner with his arms around his two girls waiting for the school bus. He was standing there, shivering with just jeans and a T-shirt on. I stopped my patrol car and said, "Man, are you crazy? What the hell are you doing out here? You're going to freeze."

He said, "Can't help it. Some bastards at school stole my girls' coats. So I gave them my stuff." His little girl had on three shirts and his other girl had on his coat. He was standing there half-naked, balancing on one leg, hugging them, keeping them warm.

Is there anything about this man that reminds you of your dad or his sacrifices for you?

I would have to say _____

_____

_____

_____.

What could you relate to in these stories about fathers?

When I was reading, I was thinking about _____

_____

_____

_____.

One of the best things my father ever did for me was _____

_____

_____.

And one of the worst things was _____

_____

_____.

In the three stories about fathers, what made me think the most about my dad was _____, because

_____

_____

_____.

I'm like him because we both _____

_____

_____,

and I'm different from him because he is _____

_____, but I am _____

_____.

One thing I learned by talking to troubled teenagers is that one of the most basic problems we have in this country is not with drugs and alcohol but with family relationships. No matter what kind of relationship you've had with your father, you need to see that relationship more clearly and learn as much as you can from it. I want you to think as hard as you can about the close and the distant times with your dad. I want you to start all the way back at the beginning and let the memories and feelings come back to you. Don't see him as either better or worse than he was.

You think about your father and who he has been in your life as carefully as possible. Memories come back to you.

You see him _____

_____

and you see him _____

_____

and you see him _____

_____

_____.

Then you say:

Dave, one of the earliest memories of my father is _____

_____

_____

_____.

Thinking about that early memory, I feel _____

_____

_____.

A clear memory from my childhood is _____

_____

_____.

Maybe I remember that so clearly because _____

_____

_____.

Other memories of him that come back to me are _____

_____

_____

_____

_____

_____

_____.

When I think of the best of times between the two of us, I remember _____

_____

_____

_____

_____

_____.

When I think of the worst of times between the two of us, I remember _____

_____

_____

_____

_____.

If you could say everything you ever wanted to say to your
dad what would it be?

I would say _____

_____

_____

_____

_____

_____

_____

_____

_____

_____

_____

_____

_____.

How does that make you feel?

Right now I feel _____

_____

_____,

because _____

_____

_____.

Now here is the most important part. Your life and your future are your own. You make your own decisions. No matter what anyone does to you or for you, the responsibility for everything you do and the credit for all you do, belongs to nobody but yourself. Everything of value you learn, you teach to yourself. Look at your relationship with your father. What can you learn by looking at the kind of father he has been?

When I look at my dad I see a man who is _____

_____

_____

_____.

What I need to learn from that is _____

_____

_____.

I need to remember this, because _____

_____
_____.

And what can you learn from looking at your relationship with him?

I look at my dad and me and I see two people who _____
_____
_____
_____.

What I need to learn from that is _____
_____
_____
_____.

This is important to remember, because _____
_____
_____
_____
_____.

Next, we'll talk about your mother.

5

Your Mother

Let's start this chapter differently from the last one. (Remember, in place of your mother you can substitute an older sister, a grandmother, an aunt, a female guardian, whoever is right for your situation.)

When you think of your mother, what are the first words that occur to you?

The first words that occur to me about my mother are _____
_____
_____.

When you think about her how do you feel?

I feel _____
_____
_____,

because _____
_____
_____.

Use those feelings as a starting place, and let me tell you some things I've heard from other teenagers about their mothers.

I remember one December in the early 1980s when I was in St. Louis. I'd talked to about fifteen hundred high-school kids in an auditorium, and they'd ended up giving me a standing ovation. After I finished talking to a lot of them in an office, I went outside for a walk in a snow-covered park. I was feeling great. Yeah, I thought, this is what I want to do with my life. A tall skinny girl, with big, dark eyes, caught up to me and this is some of what she said. "I got the worst mother on earth. I'm the oldest girl in a family of six brothers and five sisters. My mom does nothing. I cook, I clean, I wash all the kids' clothes. I practically have to fight her to get out of the door in the morning to go to school. From the seventh grade on, I've always had the worst attendance of any kid in my class. My mom treats me like a slave. And it's just getting worse. She started on drugs in the sixties and she's always smoked joints. Now she's started on meth. It's almost better when she's bombed because then I have a little freedom but I don't go anywhere. I'm afraid for my little brothers and sisters."

I told her, "If your mother is doing drugs, and you have little brothers and sisters around the house, please get to someone quick either to get your mom out of the house, to get some help, or to get the kids out of the house. You are living with a tragedy that could happen any second in many, many different ways. Get her help fast. A police officer, member of the clergy, counselor, someone. But do it now." I'm happy to say she took my advice.

Maybe you think you've got the greatest or worst mom in the world. Tell me more about her.

Dave, my mother is the kind of woman who _____
_____
_____.

The best things about her are _____
_____
_____.

The worst things about her are _____

_____

_____.

One afternoon after I'd given a lecture at a San Diego high school, a girl set up an appointment with me in the counselor's office. This was when the hip kids were really into black. She had on black clothes and heavy black eye shadow with little silver skulls for earrings. "Dave," she said, "I don't know if my mother is wonderful or crazy. All the kids envy me. She lets me do whatever I want. It's scary. I don't like it. I've come home drunk, bombed, stayed out all night, she just shrugs her shoulders and says, 'It's your life. Do what you want.' She wasn't always like this. When my mom and dad were still married, we had this really neat family. It was like a dream. We always did things together, went hiking and camping, surfing. But then my dad got involved with a woman from work and everything fell apart. I think I kind of went crazy and my mom just gave up on life. It's more like we're roommates now than mother and daughter. She doesn't care anything about what I do or say. Last night I told her to go to hell and she just said, 'I'm there.' "

I said, "Your mom is not your friend if she is allowing you to get away with all this. Your mother is going through turmoil and has thrown caution to the winds. You are allowing yourself to be destroyed by your dad's and mom's actions. Every one of us needs to be disciplined. What discipline really means is simply 'to teach.' We all need to be taught, and that's part of what love is all about. The later you come home and the more you drink, the sooner you will go down the drain. Don't destroy yourself because of her."

Maybe your mom lets you get away with everything or maybe she is too strict. Maybe you think she never lets you alone or maybe you think she doesn't pay enough attention to you.

What's your reaction to this girl's story?

My mother is _____

_____

_____

_____.

In the last chapter you described how your father was on the outside and inside, what would you say about your mom?

When people first meet my mom, they see a woman who ____

_____

_____

_____.

On the inside, I know she is _____

_____

_____.

Keep going.

My mother's goals in life are _____

_____

_____

_____.

The most important things to her right now are _____

_____

_____

_____.

The ways we are alike are _____

_____

_____.

And the ways we are different are _____

_____

_____.

I remember a boy I met in Santa Fe, New Mexico, who spent about an hour telling me all the terrible things his father had done to him and his brothers. I asked him about his mother and he just started crying. Then he said, "Dave, if it wasn't for my mom I would have killed myself. Every time my father beats me, he has to go through her. I've seen him beat her until she was unconscious, just to get to me or one of my brothers. He locks us in the bathroom so he can beat us, and she has come after him through the window! I can't count the number of times she has gotten my oldest brother out of jail. He's a heroin addict, he even stole my mother's wedding ring and sold it, and my mother forgave him. That's my mother. Pure forgiveness. When her father died, he left her some money and she sold this old junk car she had and bought a new Chevy Caprice. After she had it a week, my brother took it out and ran it into a telephone pole, totaled it. She got mad, but mostly she was mad at him because he could have killed himself. We beg and plead with her to leave my dad. She won't do it. She's been married to him for eighteen years and she remembers how he used to be. In the beginning he was a good man but he's just a drunk now. She thinks she can save him. That's the only thing wrong with her."

I told this boy, "You have to understand that millions of women go through this for many reasons. They won't leave their husbands because of the paycheck he gives them or they don't want to destroy the family or they are afraid their husbands will kill them or harm their children. Please go to Alcoholics Anonymous or Teen-Anon and listen to what other people in your situation have gone through and what they have done. Sometimes harsh actions have to be taken. You may have to call the police or go in front of a judge. But you must work on your mom over and over to do something. If what you say is true, then you are the one who has to start things going." This boy and I talked for a while longer, then I gave him a phone number he could call and helped him follow through.

Think about your mother. What are the best memories you have of her?

You think for a while.

You remember when _____
_____.

Another time you remember when _____
_____.

Dave, the very best memory I have of my mother is one time
when _____
_____
_____
_____.

This memory means so much to me, because _____
_____
_____.

Now, because we're trying to see both the bad and the good
about your life, think of the worst memories you have of your
mother.

Dave, the worst memories I have of my mother are _____
_____
_____
_____.

These are so painful because _____
_____
_____.

And what can you learn by looking at your mother?

The best things I could learn would be _____
_____
_____
_____.

Now, I'll tell you about my mom and then I'll help you see your relationship as a whole with your mother.

My mom was the greatest woman I ever knew. She was like a saint. Every Wednesday for as long as I can remember she would go down to the prisons or the reform schools or the people who were in jail and pray with them. Not long ago I met a man who had been in a coma and my mother had prayed over him for weeks. He told me, "Dave, I don't know how to explain it, but I felt your mother there. I felt her there every day. It was her prayers that pulled me through."

I remember going with her down to a bakery and buying boxes of day-old bread. We hardly had enough money to feed ourselves, but she would take this bread and go up and down the street giving it to poor families. Everywhere she went she had friends, people who knew of her goodness, people who loved her. She'd give them food, presents, but most of all her love. She was incredibly loving. She was always touching, hugging, kissing her kids. You couldn't walk by her in the kitchen, the living room, anywhere, that she wouldn't reach out to you, touch you, let you know that she loved you. She never lived for or cared about herself. Her whole mission in life was to live for others, her children, her husband, her relatives, people she met in jails, anywhere. From my mother's point of view there was no such thing as a bad person. I can remember her saying over and over again, "Dave, this person just has a problem, he's not really bad," or "Dave, don't be angry at what happened. You have to understand why people do things. No one is really bad in their heart." I never heard her raise her voice, I never saw her get mad. She was pure love.

Maybe you don't have a terrific relationship with your mother or maybe it is wonderful. Tell me one of the most loving things your mother ever did.

I remember once _____

_____

_____

_____.

And what can you teach yourself about love from that?

I should teach myself _____

_____

_____.

Now just as you did in the last chapter, I want you to think back about your relationship with your mother. Start with your earliest memories. Add other memories. Tell me about the best and the worst times. Try to see the truth about your relationship with her. Let everything you feel come out.

You think about your relationship with your mother.

You remember when _____

_____

and you remember when _____

_____

and you remember when _____

_____

_____.

Then you say:

One of the first memories of my mother is _____

_____

_____.

Thinking about that early memory, I feel _____

_____

_____.

A vivid memory from my childhood is _____

_____

_____.

Maybe I remember that so clearly, because _____

_____

_____.

Some other memories of her are _____

_____

_____

_____

_____

_____.

When I think of the greatest times between the two of us, I re-member _____

_____

_____

_____

_____

_____.

When I think of the worst of times between the two of us, I re-member _____

_____

_____

_____

_____

_____.

If you could say everything you ever wanted to say to your mom what would it be?

I would say _____

_____

_____

_____

_____

_____

_____

_____

_____

_____

_____

_____

_____

_____.

How does that make you feel?

Right now I feel _____

_____

_____,

because _____

_____

_____

_____.

Maybe you can tell already that one of the most important things you can do in our conversation is teach yourself the lessons you need to learn. I'll tell you what I have learned from others and what I know about drugs, alcohol, and other teenage problems, but you have to find the wisdom in your own life. Nobody knows you better than you. Other people have tried to tell you how to live, but now it's time for you to tell yourself. What can you learn by looking at your mother?

When I look at my mom I see a woman who is _____

_____

_____

_____.

What I need to learn from that is _____

_____

_____.

I need to remember this, because _____

_____.

And what can you learn from looking at your relationship with her?

I look at my mother and me and I see two people who _____

_____

_____

_____.

What I need to learn from that is _____

_____

_____

_____.

This is important to remember, because _____

_____.

Now, here's a story that might help you understand your parents.

6

Understanding Your Parents

A friend my age told me this recently and I'll pass it on to you.

"Dave, I could never understand my parents. They did things, acted ways I couldn't figure out. For example, take their attitude toward money. Both of them acted like it was almost holy. When I was a kid and my dad would see me stuff dollar bills into my front pocket he would get furious. I wasn't treating money with respect! Money was not something you wadded up. You smoothed out your bills and put them nicely and neatly into your billfold. My mother used to get mad when she'd come into my room and see change lying on my desk. Money was not something you left lying around. You had a special place for it, a drawer, a jar, someplace. I used to think they were so weird until I got a little older. Then something very obvious occurred to me. My dad wasn't always my dad and my mother wasn't always my mother. In fact, for most of their lives they didn't even know I was coming. It seemed very strange to think of them as people not parents. They had their own lives and experiences before I was born. I realized both of them had grown up during the Depression. When my father found work in the early thirties, there was only fifty dollars left in the whole family. When that was gone, they had no clue how they were going to survive. In the late thirties my mother arrived in Long Beach, didn't know a soul, and only had a quarter to her name! She used a nickel to buy a paper, read the want ads, and used another nickel to make a phone call and land a job as a baby-sitter. Amazing! But experiences like that were why they had such a different attitude toward money than I did. Money in the Depression *was* sacred. The more I began to think about what I knew about their lives before I was born, the more sense their actions made to me. My mother had a terrible relationship with her mother; some of that got passed on to me. My father had never been shown much affection; he had a hard time showing me affection. I began to see that they were real people, weren't perfect and needed just as much understanding as I did.''

Try this as an experiment. Pick the parent or guardian who is hardest for you to understand. Then think about everything you know about his or her past. Try to use this information to see your parent's personality more clearly.

It's worth a try. I'll pick _____. Some of the strongest influences in this parent's past were _____

_____

_____

_____

_____.

I remember hearing about _____

_____

_____

and about when _____

_____

_____

_____.

Experiences like that would probably make my parent some-one who _____

_____

_____

_____.

I've always had a hard time understanding why _____

_____

_____

_____.

Perhaps now I might explain this by saying _____

_____

_____

_____.

Good job. Now, let's try another experiment.

Look back at what you've said in this chapter and the two earlier ones about your parents. Imagine you are reading something written by another teenager. Start by giving this imaginary teenager a name.

"I'll call this imaginary teenager with a life so much like my own _____."*

What do you see in _____'s* life?

"I see a teenager who is basically _____

_____

_____.

"When I look at _____'s* feelings about _____

father I see _____

_____

_____

_____

_____.

* Fill in this name wherever there is an asterisk (*). Fill in "his" or "her" where appropriate. For example, if you picked _John_ as a name then you would fill in blanks like this: "When I look at <u>John's</u>* feelings about <u>his</u> father I see _____."

"When I look at _____'s* feelings about _____

mother I see _____

_____

_____

_____

_____.''

And what advice would you give _____*?

"I would say, 'The best thing you can do in your relationship

with your father is _____

_____

_____

_____.

'The best thing you can do in your relationship with your

mother is _____

_____

_____

_____.' ''

Don't forget that. What you just said will help guide you toward your new life. Now it's time to talk about your friends.

7

You and Your Friends

Here's a story a teenager in Seattle told me recently about himself and his friends.

"I've been hanging around with the same group of guys since about the fifth grade. There're five of us and it seems like we're always together. Every summer we played Little League and were always on the same team. We'd go swimming down at the pool, chase girls, just goof around. We'd fight, make up, hang out at each other's houses. These guys are kind of like my second family. One thing I've noticed about us, though, is that we kind of take sides against each other. We're friends but it's kind of like there's always one or two that are on the outside and the others are on the inside. It's dumb but we talk about each other. Each guy is always trying to be one of the inside ones and make somebody else one of the outsiders. This is weird because all we do is hang around together, and I can't remember one time when we were all like equals. We make ourselves feel good by making one or the other one of us feel bad. When we kid each other, it's not just playing around. We know just what to say to make the other guy feel bad. This one guy stutters so we say, 'Hey, spit it out!' Another guy is kind of fat so we make fat jokes about him, and then we act like it's his fault if he gets mad. We say this stuff kind of to stay on the attack so nobody caps on us. When I think about it, one of the main things we do when we're together is cut each other down. Each guy has his own weakness, and we know just how far to go. Sometimes it gets to be too much, and one guy will kind of like disappear or just be quiet, and then we all try to make him part of us again and then when we do, it starts all over."

I told him, "When you leave a friend and then talk about him to anyone, whether it be another friend or someone in the family, or you call someone 'fat boy' or 'skinny' or you imitate or insult a stutterer, **you** have the problem, not them. To make fun at someone else's expense shows you are very unsure of yourself and need to dwell on another person's problems to feel good about yourself. I would advise you to take a good look in the mirror. We all have our hang-ups and we all have little things to deal with whether it is a physical problem or wearing glasses or not dressing well. A friend doesn't criticize or hurt someone. He or she reaches out no matter what."

Tell me about you and your friends and anything that goes on between you that is like what this boy talked about.

Dave some of my best friends are _____
_____
_____.

The things we do together are _____
_____
_____.

The best times we have are when _____
_____
_____.

These are great times because _____
_____
_____.

The worst times are when _____

_____ _____

_____.

I don't like these times because _____

_____

_____.

When I think about my friends and what the boy from Seattle told you, I see _____

_____

_____

_____

_____.

The worst things we do to each other are _____

_____

_____.

These are bad because _____

_____

_____.

The best things we do for each other are _____

_____

_____.

We should do these more often because _____

_____

_____.

In Atlanta, I talked to students in a ghetto high school. A group of girls came up on stage afterward, and one of them, a girl with thick glasses and long hair told me this story about her and her girlfriends.

"I don't live with my friends, but I practically do. They know things about me that I would never, ever tell my parents. When I got pregnant, before I even told my boyfriend, I told my two best friends. I never even thought of telling my parents. They would have killed me. When I got an abortion, one of my best friends went with me. My other best friend's father was mad at her and wouldn't let her out of the house or she would have gone too. Boyfriends come and go but your girlfriends stay forever. We're together so much people say, 'Here come the triplets.' When one of us has a problem then we're all unhappy together. If something great happens like one of us is in love or something, then we're all happy. For Christmas we buy each other better presents than we do our own family. Our families get mad at us, but we don't care. We love each other. We hug each other. We're *together*. We always talk about running away together. We want to move to New York City and be models. We laugh about that. We'd probably end up broke and starving. We wouldn't care. We'd help each other. Each of us is going to be in the other's weddings. We've got that all planned. And our kids will play with each other's kids. And if our husbands want us to move away from each other, forget them!"

Are you and your friends similar to or different from this girl's?

Dave, I would say _____

_____

_____

_____.

When I look at the group I hang around with, I see _____

_____

_____

_____.

Basically, we are _____

_____

_____

_____.

Now pick two of your friends and describe each as clearly as you can.

I'll start with _____. This friend likes to _____

_____

_____.

This friend doesn't like to _____

_____

_____.

When I look carefully at this person, I see someone who _____

_____

_____

_____.

The worst characteristics I see are _____

_____

_____

_____.

The best characteristics I see are _____

_____

_____

_____.

We are alike because we both _____

_____

_____.

We are different because _____

_____

_____.

The second friend I'll describe is _____. This friend likes to _____
_____.

This friend doesn't like to _____
_____
_____

When I look carefully at this person, I see someone who _____
_____
_____.

The worst characteristics I see are _____
_____
_____.

The best characteristics I see are _____
_____
_____.

We are alike because we both _____
_____
_____.

We are different because _____
_____
_____.

Now here are two simple, but important lessons you can teach yourself, which will guide you toward a new life and away from your old life. First, what are the kinds of things you and your friends do that are definitely bad for you to do, that strengthen your old life? Second, what are the kinds of things you and your friends do (or could do) that are the best for you, that strengthen your new life?

The worst things we do are _____

_____

_____

_____ .

It's stupid for us to do these things, because _____

_____

_____

_____ .

The next time somebody suggests something like this, what I'll
do is _____

_____

_____

_____ .

The best things for us to do would be _____

_____

_____

_____ .

This would be good for us, because _____

_____

_____ .

What I could do to try to make this happen would be _____

_____

_____

_____ .

Step by step, you're advancing toward your new life. The next
thing we need to talk about is love.

8

Love

A good way to learn more about yourself is to think about the kind of person you fall in love with and how you act when you are in love. As you'll see from the following stories, love changes us, not always for the better.

A boy from outside Des Moines told me about the first time he fell in love. "Dave, I live way out in what you would call the boonies. There is nothing to do in my little town in the summer except go to the park and watch baseball games. I met this girl there, Cheryl, she was on the girl's softball team. I guess I should say she met me. My friends tease me because I'm so shy. If Cheryl hadn't come up to me, I never would have had the nerve to talk to her. I want to talk. I want to be open but something just keeps me from it. It's because I think too much about what I'm going to say, and I'm like outside of myself looking at myself instead of just talking or being natural. I feel like everything I do is an act. After Cheryl talked to me I went down to the park every time she had a game and she would stop by and talk to me and I would act like it was no big deal, but it was all I thought about all week. Then she said why didn't I come over to her family's house on the Fourth of July and I said I'd try to make it. I said this like I was such a busy guy! I drove by her house about five times just hoping she would come out and about the sixth time she did. She wanted to know why I drove by so many times, was I lost? I just kind of laughed. What could I say? Then she said, 'Let's go in,' and I said no. And she could tell I was shy, so she pulled me by the hand and made me follow her and she held my hand all the way through the gate, past where she had to. I was sixteen, that was the first time I ever held a girl's hand. We got inside and everybody said hi and they treated me like I was this important guy. I started dreaming like crazy, thinking, wondering, has she been talking about me and it felt too good to be true. That night we watched her dad and her brothers set off bottle rockets and Roman candles in the backyard and we just sat side by side together on the porch swing and her little sister was climbing in and out of my lap. I just sat there with my side touching Cheryl's side and that was the first of the great moments of our relationship.

"We started going out together and we never did anything. Just got hamburgers at McDonald's, went to the show, drove around to my friends' and her friends' houses, but it was like heaven. We could have just picked gravel out of the tires and it would have been great. There's this field in the back of my uncle's place and a pond back there and we used to go back there and just sit on the hill and look at the stars. I had an astronomy class my sophomore year and this made me seem like a brain. I was so shy she always had to take my hand and put it over her shoulder. She called me Ice Man. About the third night we were out by the pond she said, 'Don't you know you're my favorite person?' I wanted to get up and do somersaults. She put her head on my shoulder and I was so shy it was all I could do to lean my cheek over into her hair and then we ended up rubbing cheeks together. Then we turned our faces and kissed. I can remember how it felt to have my face so close to her face. I wanted to get married.

"When school started everything changed. I came up to her after first period and she was standing with a bunch of her friends and she and I started to walk away together and I could tell right away she didn't want to hold hands. Her arm just sort of hung down straight and that was all she had to do. I was so mad I couldn't talk. Then she said, 'What's wrong?' and I said, 'Nothing's wrong,' and then we went back and forth like that and then she said, 'Well, maybe I'll see you at lunch.' One word can kill a person. It was that word *maybe* that killed me. So, of course, I didn't go into the cafeteria at lunch and then the next day I couldn't even look at her. Now every time I see her at school it's so embarrassing it kills me. I pretend like she is nothing to me and she pretends the same and that's it for my first romance."

Can you see yourself in any part of this boy's story?

I think _____

_____

_____.

Have you ever been this shy?

When I like somebody I feel _____

_____

_____.

I act _____,

because _____

_____.

Tell me about the first time you were in love.

I remember _____

_____

_____

_____

_____

_____

_____

_____

_____.

Look back on that first love relationship. What can you teach yourself?

A good lesson would be _____

_____

_____.

Here's another love story. This one is from a girl in San Francisco who had dropped out of school to work at Carl's Jr.

"I guess you could say I'm wild. If there's a group of kids doing things I'm the instigator. I just have this energy inside me that wants to be wild. It's not hard to get me excited. That's what everyone has always told me all my life, calm down. I don't want to be calm. I want to be me. I noticed this tall, cute guy coming in to get a hamburger every day for lunch. He went to San Francisco University. He had on a sweatshirt one day from there so that's what I guessed. He'd always asked for a hamburger and I always asked would he want fries with that or a salad or a brownie—just joking around to get him to notice me. Every night I'd go home dreaming about this guy, I told all my girlfriends about him, he seemed so wonderful.

"About the third time he came in, he said why didn't we go for a drive after I got off work. I'm wild, but I'm not crazy. I said no thanks. Then the next day he said why didn't we go out to eat dinner someplace, and I said okay. I knew, of course, that this was something my dad wouldn't go for. After I dropped out of high school I was on kind of semipermanent restriction. I could only go out with people he knew to places he knew about, and it was hell. So I told my girlfriend to call me and invite me over to help baby-sit her brother and she did and so I went out with this guy. I was so nervous! He was twenty-one and I was seventeen. I had no idea how somebody that old acted. Whatever he said I just tried to fit in with that. He was a basketball fan from L.A. and so we talked about the Lakers and I made it seem like basketball was my favorite thing. Boy, I just lived for basketball on TV. He was also studying engineering and I've never had a clue what that was, but I was so stupid I didn't ask him. Guys love to tell you about what you don't know. He took me to Fisherman's Wharf. We had this dinner that cost about twenty bucks apiece, I could tell he was kind of shocked at how much it came to in the end. Then we went walking and it was so cold I just kind of snuggled up to him and he opened his coat and I got in under his arm and we just stood against the fence looking out at the Bay talking about Magic Johnson. I had my arms around him inside his coat and I thought is this guy Mr. Basketball Encyclopedia? He wasn't seeming that cute to me and then we started kissing and it was okay, he was what I would call a wood-pecker kisser. Kind of pecked you on the lips with his lips instead of staying there. He'd kiss me and look at me and then kiss me again and I didn't know what the looking was for. Then he took me home that night and all the way home we were kissing at the stop-lights, kissing in traffic, but then when I got home I knew I didn't want to see him anymore.

"That's the way I am. I love somebody until I meet them. Then everything I feel goes away and I wonder what I was up to and then somebody new comes along and I'm crazy about them."

Have you ever felt like this girl or known anyone like her?

Dave, _____
_____
_____
_____ .

Is there anything you can learn about yourself from this girl's story?

I would have to say _____
_____
_____
_____ .

Tell me about a disappointing love experience.

I remember when _____

_____

_____

_____

_____

_____

_____

_____

_____.

What can you learn about yourself from that?

I should remember _____

_____

_____.

Here is another love story. I'll never forget this girl. After I lectured at a New York City high school, I was sitting down in the cafeteria and she brought her lunch and sat down next to me. She was crying. We talked for a while and this is what she told me.

"I don't know what's wrong with me. I can't get over breaking up with my boyfriend. I feel empty inside. I can't believe this is happening to me. I never used to be like this. Before I met him I was just your normal, average teenager. I had troubles with my parents but never anything major. I play the trumpet, which is kind of weird for a girl, but there's something weird about everyone. I met him at a football game. I was sitting with my friends and he and his friends came and sat behind us and he kept tapping me on the shoulder and asking me silly questions, like would I explain the game to him. How many points did you get for a touchdown? Who was the man in the striped shirt? This guy just had this funny way about him and he was extremely good looking. His other friends were talking with my girlfriends, but he was the cutest of any of his friends and everything he said was just so funny. I found out he went to this other high school and I thought I would never see him again and then two days later he was sitting on the stairs up to our apartment and he had this stuffed panda bear in his arms and said I had left it at the football game. This was so great. I thought I'd never see him again and then there he was out of nowhere just sitting there with this stuffed bear. He said all this funny stuff about how he and the bear had to track me down and I was cracking up, and it was just the easiest thing talking to him. My dad came out and he talked to my dad like it was nothing. Nobody had ever done that. Before long he was cracking jokes with my dad about Mayor Koch. He did an imitation of Koch that was a crack-up. My dad said why didn't he come in and have a soda and this was just amazing. My dad never invites anybody I know in. He came in and started talking to my brothers and stayed all afternoon and when he left it was like he was already part of the family.

"Half the time when we dated we would just sit on my couch and watch TV, and even my mother liked him and she didn't even like my girlfriends. One thing everybody in my family liked was that he had a job but he was staying in school too. He worked about thirty hours a week at a gas station, and this made it hard to see him but I was totally in love. Sometimes I'd just go down to where he worked and sit in my car just so I could talk to him for a few minutes every hour. I'd do my homework in the car and maybe sit there three or four hours. Then one day one of my girlfriends said she saw him downtown with this girl I hate. I couldn't believe it. I didn't believe it. I'm not someone to keep things inside. I went up to him and told him what I'd heard and he said it was a lie so I believed him and not my girlfriend. I actually broke up with her about this. Then my brother went to a dance at a high school on the other side of the city and saw him with another girl. I went to him and asked what was going on and he said, 'Oh she's just a friend.' This made me angry but he was so good at controlling my feelings, I forgave him in about two hours. Then it seemed like things weren't going that well between us but this made me just cling onto him more. I had a chance to go to Florida over Easter, but I didn't go just because I wanted to be with him and all we did was spend an afternoon shopping for his father's birthday present. The rest of the time he was 'busy.'

"Now here is the part I can't believe. I actually went and tried to spy on him. I guess I was kind of going crazy. I've never been the jealous or insecure type but there was something about this guy that really, really got to me. He was the first guy I've ever really, truly loved. I never found him with anyone. Then one day I was at his house and he was in the shower and this girl called up and I could just tell from her tone of voice that something was going on. She wanted to know who I was and I wanted to know who she was and we practically had a fight over the phone. So when he got out of the shower, I asked him about this girl, and he said he had no idea who it could be. I'm telling you I was so stupid. And he had me believing this and then about half an hour later there was a knock at the door and it was this girl coming over. She was fat! She wanted to fight me! I told her to get lost, I told him to get lost, I screamed at him and then I ran home. That was four weeks ago. I've cried every night since. If this is love, I hate it. I would kill myself except he wouldn't care."

I told this girl, "From time to time we all meet someone who we feel we are in love with and we can't live without. This is especially true when we are teenagers. But if this guy was seeing other girls, then he didn't love you enough to make a full commitment, and no matter what you feel for him, this was a one-sided love affair. As much as you hurt now, you are far better getting out of this relationship. Do you really want to love someone who you know is using you as one of many girls in his stable? No one respects someone who hangs on no matter how they are treated. If you want to cry that's okay. Don't feel bad about crying, that will just make you feel worse! But the pain will pass and there will be many more men in your life. No one is worth your destroying yourself or even thinking of killing yourself. Get out and meet other people and make sure he knows that you will not hang on and be one of his playmates."

Is there anything in this girl's story that you can identify with?

This story reminds me of _____

_____

_____

_____

_____

_____

_____

_____.

    Now think about one love relationship you were in. Think as clearly as you can about how it began and what attracted you to the other person. How did you feel? How did you act? What were some of the best times together? What were some of the worst? Try to see the relationship as clearly as you can and then try to learn a lesson about love from your experience.

    Dave, I want to tell you about me and _____. Some of my earliest memories are when _____

_____.

    I felt _____ and I thought _____.

    One of the first times we talked was when _____

_____.

    What happened was _____

_____.

    When I look at who the two of us were in the first stage of our relationship, I see two people who _____

_____

_____

_____.

    What was important to me was _____

_____ and what

was important to _____ was_____

_____.

One of the best times we ever had was when _____

_____.

What happened on that great time was _____

_____

_____

_____

_____

_____

_____

_____.

Other memories I have of the relationship are _____

_____

_____

_____

_____

_____

_____

_____

_____

_____

_____.

During this relationship I changed from someone who was

_____

to someone who was _____

_____.

I can see now that when I am in love I can become _____

_____,

probably because _____

_____.

The best lesson I could teach myself by looking at this whole relationship is _____

_____

_____.

I must remember this because _____

_____.

Every chapter is giving you more insight and taking you closer to your new life. Now let's talk about your dreams and goals.

This seems like a good time to take a break and talk a little bit about a fact of life. Most of the millions of kids I have spoken to over the years are sexually active, especially if they are doing drugs. Today, as always, being sexually active means risking pregnancy, but it also means that you are exposing yourself to sexually transmitted diseases (STDs). Most people are unaware that more than 12 million people (that we know of) from kids to executives get STDs every year. There are more than 25 different STDs (including the deadliest—AIDS), and many of these diseases destroy your body, from your reproductive organs to your brain. STDs *are* a fact of life, and if you are sexually active, you are at risk!

You hear a lot about people contracting AIDS from unsterilized needles, but this is minor compared to the number of kids and adults who are sexually active and taking their chances without protection. We must come down heavy and admit that the only sure way to protect yourself is *DON'T DO IT.* But if you are having sex with anyone, know what you can do to be safe. And you better know (and trust) the other person really well. Remember though, even then you can't be sure.

If you have questions about pregnancy, sexually transmitted diseases, or anything else related to sexual activity, please check the listing for Planned Parenthood on page 211.

Dreams and Dreamers

In this chapter I'll start by telling you about three dreamers I've known and then tell you what I think are the right and wrong ways of dreaming.

In the early seventies I was in Texas and a counselor in a high school introduced me to "the worst girl we've had in twenty years." In her three years in high school she had been in countless fights, been in and out of reform school, been through ten foster homes, and seemed well on her way to becoming a lifetime criminal. Her probation officer had a list of more than forty arrests, ranging from petty theft to prostitution. If she hadn't been so young—she was only seventeen—she would have been in the penitentiary.

Call her Janet. She sat slouched down in her chair with an expression that said Get lost. I tried talking and she just looked at me with dark angry eyes and wouldn't say anything. I was just another adult and adults meant nothing but trouble. I worked hard and finally got her to talk a little. Everything she said was negative. She hated everybody. She hated herself. Everyone was against her. She would be better off dead.

I tried to find some spark, something inside her that was positive which she could hang onto. I finally got her to admit that when she was a girl everyone had praised her for her singing. I asked her who she admired. She named a few famous female singers. I got her to talk about why she admired these women and she began to open up a little. Then maybe I got lucky, but I'd rather think God helped me. Because I wasn't up to date on the latest music, I asked if she ever listened to any of the "oldies but goodies." She said one of the women she admired the most was a singer from the seventies who, it turned out, was a close friend of mine. I went over to the phone and called this woman. She'd told me she'd just finished a long road trip the week before. We talked for a while and then I told her Janet's story and asked her to talk to her. As soon as Janet recognized her voice, she couldn't believe it. Her face broke open into this huge smile and then she started talking a mile a minute.

I just went outside and waited. After about an hour, Janet came out beaming and said what they talked about was dreams. My friend told her about struggling for fifteen years before she ever cut her first record, how record producers and agents had cheated her for years, how she'd been so low she'd gotten involved in drugs, but she had never lost her dream. By the end of the conversation, Janet said she couldn't keep from crying. My friend had touched her heart and helped her to start looking for her own dreams.

I know I'm not exaggerating when I say that phone call changed Janet's life. I met her ten years later and she was one of the hottest record producers in the South and had just signed a four-year development deal with a major record company.

"Dave," she told me, "I was as far down as a person could be. Everything was dark. I hated the world. I didn't have anything to live for, nothing to shoot for. I was seventeen and ready to jump off the nearest bridge. After that phone call, I thought, maybe I can do something in music too. It wasn't easy and I made plenty of mistakes and almost lost it all more times than I can count, but I made something of myself I can be proud of. I never made it as a singer, but I did get a few jobs as backup. But the dream of singing led me to another one, working in sound studios, and that dream led to me another one, being a record producer. It all started with looking for my dream."

Take a few moments now and tell me what you really want out of life.

Dave, some of my dreams are _____

_____

_____

_____

_____.

What I want from life is _____.

_____

_____.

It would be great if somebody _____

_____

_____.

Look at dreams from a different angle. What could you do that would make you really proud of yourself?

I would love it if I could _____

_____

_____.

This would be great because _____

_____

_____.

Now tell me about someone you really admire.

A person I really look up to is _____, because

_____

_____.

If I were going to try to be more like this person, the first thing I would do would be _____,

because _____
_____.

Other things I would do would be _____
_____
_____.

Here's the story of another dreamer who might inspire you.

At fourteen, Kevin, an inner-city kid from Detroit, was deeply involved with drugs. He was making six hundred dollars a week working as a runner for the leader of a neighborhood gang. Unfortunately one summer night, Kevin was in the wrong place at the wrong time. A rival gang came cruising through, and two shotgun blasts crippled him from the neck down. When I met him five years later he weighed about ninety pounds, had to use his chin on a special device to guide his wheelchair and, I have to say, was one of the happiest people I've ever met. He spent all his time going around to elementary schools talking to students about drugs and gangs and, you guessed it, dreams. Just to impress kids, he'd developed a special ability to do complex math word problems in his head. He'd challenge his audience to use calculators and he'd whip out answers faster than anyone. He explained a few tricks to me that he'd learned from a gifted math teacher who had inspired him. I didn't quite understand what he was saying, but I loved the fire in his eyes. He was so proud and confident and full of life. I watched him talk to a fourth-grade class about the life he'd had as drug runner and then how he'd thought his life was ruined after he got shot. He'd gone through six operations and they'd all failed. Some of the kids cried as he spoke to them. Then he talked about how he had prayed and prayed that God take his life, how he wished he could die but didn't. Then he'd met a math teacher and little by little he'd found himself able to do things he'd never imagined he could. Then the teacher suggested he go to a local school and talk to the kids about his experiences . . . and after that there was no looking back. His goal was to get his Ph.D. in math no matter how long it took and then go teach in a ghetto school. An idiot with a gun had crippled his body, but hadn't touched his dreams. He finished by telling everyone his "secret." The secret was simply this: All his life he had heard a little voice that said, "No you can't." After he got shot he heard that voice day and night, "No you can't. No you can't." The secret he said, was **don't listen.** "That little voice is a liar," he said, and the whole class stood up and applauded him because they knew he was right.

Now, let's talk about some of the things that you tell yourself that keep you from dreaming.

Sometimes when I think about some really great future I destroy it by thinking _____

_____

_____

_____.

My own little voice says _____

_____

_____.

What should you say back?

The next time I'll say _____

_____

_____.

What could you do tomorrow to start toward one of your goals?

I could _____

_____.

What else could you do?

I could _____

_____.

And what will you do when you try to talk yourself out of even trying?

I'll _____

_____

_____ .

What will be the most enjoyable part of trying to make your dreams come true?

I'd have to say _____

_____

_____ .

Great! Enjoy it!

I met a girl in east Los Angeles not very long ago who told me the following story. "I was born in MexiCali just across the border from California. The whole time I was growing up, I'd look through the fence and it didn't look that different from where I lived, just sand and dirt but I thought if I'd been born in the U.S., just a mile from my home, that my life would be a lot better. When I was nine, I came to Los Angeles with my parents and grandparents. My mother got a job in the garment district, and my father did the best he could with day labor. I learned English as fast as I could because I knew that's what I needed to get ahead. Life in L.A. was better than in MexiCali, but not that much better. We ate mostly beans and tortillas and for Christmas we'd be lucky if we all got one present each. Every day after school my brothers and sisters and I would scrounge through trash cans for aluminum cans, and we had to be fast because there were grown men who were trying to get them too. One summer we made ninety dollars just with cans. Then my oldest brother got the idea of washing cars, and so we would go around door to door and charge a dollar a car and a dollar and a half for a big pickup. We did good work and built up a little business in about three square miles around our house. Then my mother taught me and my older sister to sew. She would bring work home and we would sew pockets on shirts. We could make about two dollars an hour which was more than we could make washing cars. It's funny but when I was in Mexico I don't remember working that much, but since I came to the U.S. it seems like all I do is go to school and work. It's probably because I'm getting older and I can make money to help my family out.

"This will sound silly, but my big dream is to have my own dog. I want a big, beautiful collie, but the kind I want, costs over two hundred dollars. His name is going to be Berto. I give most of my money to my family, but I have a little money of my own saved now. I know if I keep working I'll have enough to buy him. I like to dream about things I can get on my own."

There are good and bad ways to dream. You can lay in your bed and have fantasies about being the richest, most powerful and attractive person in the world and get up feeling terrible because your real life is impossibly far from your dream. The wrong kind of dreaming makes you feel miserable, defeated, powerless when the dream is over. The wrong kinds of dreams are about things you cannot achieve on your own. For example, let us say your dream is to be a world famous rocker. In order for that to happen millions of people have to buy into your dream. Agents, record producers, and the media not to mention a world full of fans all have to support your fantasy. Not only is this a bad dream because you need too many people to make it come true but also because when you stop dreaming you feel miserable. You feel miserable because everyone is ignoring you. You have no clue how to make the world love you. A much better plan would be to dream about learning to play the guitar fantastically well. You don't need anyone to follow this dream. Nobody on earth can stop you from practicing. Even if your parents hated the electric guitar, you would only have to go where they couldn't hear you. And when you stop dreaming the good dream of learning to play the guitar incredibly well, it is very clear what you could do to begin to make this dream a reality. You don't need an agent or bookings or fans. The first steps are obvious. Get a part-time job, save a little money, buy a guitar, find a teacher. Practice would be great because you would be realizing your goal. Dreaming about learning how to play the guitar incredibly well is a great dream because you can strive for it *on your own power*. Every minute you spend with your fingers on the strings will take you closer and closer to mastering your instrument. Every week of practice would be its own payoff. You don't have to wait twenty years to be happy.

Remember, I'm not just lucky to be where I am. I had dreams too—dreams of being on TV, in the movies, and writing books—and I have been knocked down and dragged more times than I can count. But I kept trying, and here I am. I wanted it badly, and I got it. You have to want it, too.

The best kind of dreams are the ones you can start on immediately. You could spend the rest of your life dreaming about the fame and the possessions of a world-famous rocker and never be anything but miserable because you're not famous and rich. Or you could dream about your hands flying up and down the neck of the guitar, and every hour you would see yourself getting better and better.

Try practicing what I just described.

Start with a foolish dream that you would need a lot of other people to make come true.

Okay, Dave I'll imagine myself as a _____

_____. I see _____

_____

_____.

This is the kind of bad dream you were talking about, because

_____

_____

_____.

Now, dream about something you could start on tomorrow. What do you really want to be or do, that you could start working toward immediately?

A good dream for me would be _____

_____

_____.

Some of the things I could do to pursue this dream are _____

_____

_____

_____.

If I really want this I have to remember _____

_____ _____

_____.

The difference between this dream and the other one is _____

_____

_____

_____.

You've come a long way and worked hard. It's time for something simple.

The Best Times

This should be an easy chapter for you. I want you just to think about the greatest times you ever had. Think about birthdays, Christmases, summer vacations. Think about things you did with your family or friends. Or maybe one of the best times you ever had was something you did by yourself.

You think about _____ and about

_____ and about

_____.

When were you the happiest? Can you remember a time when you laughed so hard that you couldn't stop? How about when you had so much fun you didn't want the day to end?

You remember _____ and

you remember _____.

Was there a movie or television program you saw that really moved you? Or a concert you went to that was fantastic?

Right now you are thinking about _____

_____. You remember when _____

_____.

You remember _____

_____.

That's a beginning. Now think back over your whole life. Let the good memories return to you. Think about close times with people you love. It could just be a small moment you'll never forget or something that made you so happy that you couldn't believe it was happening. Let the memories return. Feel the joy in them.

Dave, the first thing I remember was when _____

_____.

The picture I see in my mind right now is _____

_____

_____.

I feel _____, because _____

_____.

Another great time in my life was when _____

_____

_____.

This was great because _____

_____

_____.

Let the memories come to you in any order. Let one memory lead to another. Take your time! Remember the big events and the small, let the happy times of your life come back to you.

Okay, Dave, I'll start with _____

_____

_____.

Other happy times were _____

_____

_____

_____

_____

_____

_____

_____

_____

_____

_____

_____

_____

_____

_____.

Think about your life right now. Some of the things you are doing in your life will be wonderful to remember in years to come. You are doing some things right now that are very good for you to do. They bring you true happiness; they make you feel really good inside. What are they?

The best things I am doing right now are _____

_____

_____.

They make me feel _____,
because I know _____
_____.

Now look at everything you've written in this chapter. What could you do today or tomorrow that would bring you the same happy, healthy emotions?

That's a great question, Dave! I could _____
_____
_____
_____
_____
_____
_____
_____
_____.

Congratulations! That's an important step toward a new life! In the next chapter I'll help you sum up everything you've learned so far.

11

Looking Back

It's time for you to sum up what you've taught yourself thus far in our conversation. Look back at what you've written; read again some of the stories by other teenagers that you identified with. What lesson or lessons have you learned that will guide you to your new life? Look at each chapter and write down what you want to remember.

In the third chapter I tried opening up. When I look at what I wrote there, what I need to remember is _____

_____

_____

_____.

In the fourth chapter I talked to you about my father. The best lessons I learned were _____

_____

_____

_____.

Then we talked about my mother. What I want to remember is

_____

_____

_____.

Then I spent some time thinking about my relationships with my friends. The best lessons in that chapter were _____

_____

_____

_____.

Then we talked about love. I need to learn some important lessons about that! I should remember _____

_____

_____

_____.

The next topic was dreams and goals. What I look at what I wrote, I see the best lessons were _____

_____

_____

_____.

Finally, you told me to let all my happy memories return. What I learned was _____

_____

_____

_____.

When you look at what you have written thus far what do you see?

I see a person who _____

_____

_____

_____.

I see a person who values _____

_____

_____

_____.

The strengths I see are _____

_____

_____

_____.

The weaknesses I see are _____

_____

_____

_____.

Now, give yourself your best advice about finding a new life.

What I need to do more of is _____

_____

_____

_____.

What I have to stop doing is _____

_____

_____

_____.

What I'm going to do instead is _____

_____

_____

_____.

The best advice I have to give myself about finding my new life
is _____

_____

_____.

Listen carefully to what you just said and you're on your way!

Now that you've seen your life and your relationships more clearly,
we're going to be dealing with some of the most serious problems
teenagers face. The second part of our conversation will be different
from the first. The next seven chapters, "Self-Hatred," "Destructive
Anger at Others," "Depression," "Suicidal Feelings," "Alcohol,"
"Drugs," and "Satanism" are presented as if you suffered from each
of these problems. Read and carefully complete any of the chapters
that apply to your life. Find someplace quiet to work at the rate that
is best for you. If it takes you a day or a week to complete a few
pages, then that is fine. That's the pace you should be working at.
If your feelings are churning and you can't write fast enough then
stay up all night and let it all come out. Share what you are writing
with others if that will help. You may know an adult or friend
whose advice you trust. Use the following chapters to let someone
else help you. Or you may gain insights that will help others solve
their problems. For many teenagers, one of the best things they can
do to help themselves is to help others.

All of the material in the following chapters will not apply to
you. Carefully complete the chapters that help you see your life
more clearly, and simply read the others to learn more about their
subjects.

Part 2

Seven Big Problems

12

Self-Hatred

It's normal to have negative thoughts about yourself. Everyone does. Being down on yourself occasionally is no big deal. But there is a big difference between occasionally feeling bad about who you are and having such dark, negative feelings about yourself that you don't seem able to escape them. There is a difference between self-criticism and self-hatred. Self-criticism is short term and can lead to positive results, self-hatred goes on and on and drags you farther and farther down into darkness. If your bad feelings about yourself last for days on end, if you feel bad about yourself far more often than you feel good, if your negative emotions seem out of control and seem to have a life of their own, then you should read this chapter carefully.

It might be that more teenagers' lives are ruined **by how they feel about themselves** than by drugs, alcohol, or any terrible relationship. One good way for you to see the bad things you do to yourself and the good things you could be doing to yourself, is to imagine that you have two tapes that you play in your head. One is negative and the other is positive. When you are playing the negative tape, nothing but black, self-defeating thoughts go through your mind. Your anger, your bitterness, your self-hatred, your frustration play over and over again on this tape. When you're really down, this tape plays from the moment you wake up in the morning until you go to bed at night.

There is, however, another set of thoughts which go through your mind. On the positive tape you tell yourself good things about yourself, about your past and your future, about people you know. Affirmative, confident thoughts go through your brain over and over. When you've got this tape playing, no drug on earth could make you higher.

Each of these tapes has two parts. You tell yourself negative and positive things about yourself and negative and positive things about others.

Playing the negative tape about yourself leads to self-hatred. Playing the positive tape about yourself leads to self-love.

Playing the negative tape about others leads to feelings of isolation, playing the positive tape about others leads to feelings of closeness.

In this chapter we'll concentrate on what you tell yourself about yourself and in the next chapter we'll focus on what you tell yourself about others.

You need to learn what your negative tape sounds like. You need to see what you do to yourself and you need to see **that you can turn it off.** One of the easiest parts of the negative tape to hear is what you tell yourself about how you look. When you're really down on your appearance what do you say to yourself?

I say I can't stand _____

_____

_____

_____.

Now, play more of that negative tape. What do you say to yourself that really makes you feel like a loser?

I say _____

_____

_____

_____.

Keep going. Maybe you've been doing this for years. What do you say to yourself when you hate yourself?

I say I hate myself because _____

_____

_____

_____.

Now, imagine a day when you have this negative tape playing nonstop. You've got the volume turned way up and from morning until night, all you can hear is negative, unending self-hatred. Start by imagining yourself on a typical depressed morning.

Okay, Dave, I'm glad I'm just pretending! On a normal morning what I usually do is _____

_____

_____.

Now, I'll imagine I have the negative tape playing. I wake up, and the negative thoughts I think are _____

_____

_____.

I go in to the kitchen, and I am feeling _____

_____

_____.

I look outside, and things look _____

_____

_____.

I go into the bathroom and stare in the mirror. I have my negative tape playing so when I look at myself, I see _____

_____

_____.

By this time I am feeling _____

_____

_____.

Now describe the rest of your depressed day.

I see myself at school _____,
and I am feeling _____.

Now I'm standing with some of my friends, and my negative
tape is saying _____

_____

_____.

The next thing I see myself doing is _____

_____

_____,
and I'm feeling _____.

After school what I would probably do is _____

_____

_____.

By that night if I was really depressed, really hating myself,
I would _____

_____

_____

_____.

Now listen carefully. If you keep playing that tape you're going
to have countless more days just like that one. Only week by week

and month by month, they'll keep getting worse. The negative tape keeps getting louder and louder and darker and darker. If you haven't already, the chances are that you'll do something really stupid like try to drown the tape out with drugs and alcohol. And if you *have* tried to drown it out with drugs and alcohol, then you know the truth. These poisons only make the tape louder until it is almost deafening. The next step is obvious. You can't stand the hell in your mind. And so you turn for relief . . . to death. Your inner sickness is so terrible, the only cure seems to be killing yourself. Am I saying anything you can relate to?

Dave, _____

_____

_____

_____.

Right now I'm feeling _____

_____

_____.

Listen. Don't you see what the answer is? At the very start of this chapter I asked you to turn on the tape. And you did. **The tape is under your control.** I'm not saying it is easy to control, you've had the damned thing going for years. I'm not saying it's a snap to turn off. You must know it is a lot easier to get it turned on than to get it turned off. So here is something you need to understand. **The easiest time for you to turn the negative tape off is the instant it starts playing.** The longer you let it play during the day, the harder it is to stop. You've only got two choices, stop it before it gets rolling or feel like crap. The choice is yours. Are you truly sick of feeling sick?

The truth is _____

_____

_____.

If you just said you're tired of feeling sick, then get ready to do some hard work that will help you feel better. If you're not ready to work hard, skip the rest of this chapter because just reading the words won't do you any good.

Listen to me. People are depressed about many different things: how they feel about themselves, things that have happened in their lives, how other people treat them. **But all depressed people feel alone in the world . . . and they are wrong.** Other people are going through what you are going through right now. I know you've heard this before and maybe you've shrugged it off. But let it sink in. One of the most effective ways to combat depression is to realize that your feelings are not unique, you are not on some kind of emotional desert island. Other people have the terrible emotions you are having right now. Other people have triumphed over negative emotions that were as strong and stronger than the ones you have now. **If you can conquer your feeling of isolation, then you are well on the road to victory.**

Dave, I believe _____

_____

_____.

Work hard with me now. Look at your life. Tell me the names of some people who love you.

Dave, I know people who do love me. I am thinking right now of _____

_____

_____.

Think of one who loves you right now. Think of his or her concern and love. Do it!

I am thinking of _____.
I know they feel _____. They see goodness in me.
They see I am someone who _____

_____.

Fantastic! Now imagine you have God's eye view of the whole human race. You can see all the people in the world who are suffering from depressions just like yours. What do you see?

I see that I am not alone. I see that no matter how isolated I feel, many people are going through something like what is happening to me. I see _____

_____.

The things that cause me to feel bad like _____

_____

_____

are really things that many people suffer from. **I'm not weird!** Like other people, I'm someone who _____

_____.

Now, let's keep going.

Here are three ways to stop your negative tape when it starts to play.

- Ignore what it says.
- Do something about what it says.
- Shut it down with positive messages.

The easiest messages to ignore on your negative tape are the parts that you know aren't true. Start controlling your negative tape by turning off the lies. Think about the things you tell yourself about yourself that you know aren't true.

One thing I tell myself sometimes is that I'm _____

_____

_____.

I know this isn't true because _____

_____

_____.

What's another lie you tell yourself about yourself?

Another lie is _____

_____

_____.

I know this is a lie because _____

_____

_____.

Exaggerations are another kind of lie. Let's say you tell your-self, "I'm the dumbest kid in the universe," or "I'm a zero," or "Everybody hates me." Imagine you heard someone saying these things. You would know they were way off the deep end. What are some negative exaggerations about yourself that you hear on your tape?

One negative thing that I exaggerate is _____

_____

_____.

The truth is _____

_____

_____.

Tell me something else you tell yourself that you know is an exaggeration.

When I'm feeling really depressed, something else I exaggerate is _____

_____

_____.

You've had a little practice in filtering out the negative tape by ignoring the lies and the exaggerations. Another tactic would be to do something about what the negative tape is saying. Maybe it's not lying or exaggerating. Maybe some of what it says is something you should be doing something about. Imagine you say to yourself, "I'm no good at anything." An obvious answer would be to figure out what you want to be good at and start learning. Or imagine yourself saying, "I'm rotten to my brother." An obvious answer would be to go do something nice for him. Or imagine you say to yourself, "I've got no future." Do something about it. Go talk to somebody who can give you good advice. Lie in bed and dream the good dreams we talked about in an earlier chapter. Maybe your future is taking things you learned in this book and teaching them to others. Great! But when the negative tape starts playing, cancel it by making a plan to do something.

One negative thing I say to myself that maybe I should do something about is _____
_____
_____ .

What I could do is _____
_____
_____ .

Another negative thing I say to myself is _____
_____
_____ .

What I could do about that is _____
_____
_____ .

Try one more time. Of everything you tell yourself that is negative about yourself, what would be the easiest to change?

I would say _____

_____

_____

_____.

    Besides ignoring and doing something about what the negative tape says, you could also shut it down by playing the positive tape. In fact, if you put the right things on your positive tape, then it will be much harder for the negative tape to even start!

    If you look at your friends, your teachers, your parents, anyone, you can see both good and bad in them. It's obvious. No one is completely good or completely bad. We all have our strengths and weaknesses. Your problem might be that you concentrate on some of your weaknesses, or exaggerate others, or invent others with lies or do nothing about the ones you could correct. But turn to your positive qualities. You've spent some time in the darkness, turn to the light. Tell yourself the honest truth about your strengths. What are your talents? Who do you show love to? What have you gotten praise for? What do you like about yourself? Here is the challenge. _Don't go further in this book until you've told yourself five true, positive things about yourself._ And I'll give you the first one for free. You're a good person because you're trying to solve, and not run away from, your own problems.

    Thanks, Dave! Second, I am a good person because _____

_____

_____.

    Third, I am a good person because _____

_____

_____.

    Fourth, I am a good person because _____

_____

_____.

    Fifth, I am a good person because _____

_____

_____.

Now, look at that list. There are some positive truths about you. Practice turning on one of them to silence your negative tape.

Sounds good. One negative thing I say to myself is _____

_____

_____.

And the positive thing I could tell myself instead is _____

_____

_____.

Here's some more material for your positive tape. Just look back through all you've written in this book. You've taken positive steps toward your new life again and again. Add any of them to your tape.

Some of the lessons I could repeat to myself are _____

_____

_____

_____.

And I could always say, I am a good person because I work hard at teaching myself what I need to know.

Right! Look back at chapter nine. You dreamed some good, realistic dreams. Add those to your tape.

When I wake up in the morning I could dream the good dream about _____

_____

_____

_____

_____.

When I get too down on myself, I could counter this with my positive goal of _____

_____

_____

_____.

In chapter eleven you summed up each of the lessons you needed to teach yourself about your own personality and your relationships. Add some of those lessons now to your tape.

When I start feeling negative about myself, I can say _____

_____

_____

_____

_____

_____

_____.

Now, put everything together and repeat what you've said. Make your positive tape loud and clear.

First, I'm going to repeat what I said and really let it sink in. Then, I'm going to add a special message. The things I've said in this chapter that I'm going to put onto my positive tape are

_____

_____

_____

_____

_____

_____

_____

_____.

The special message I have for myself that I should never forget
is _____

_____

_____

_____.

Think about the progress you've made in our conversation so
far. Do you feel yourself finding your new life?

Dave, the truth is _____

_____

_____.

Right now I feel _____

_____

_____.

If you've worked hard in this chapter, then you've made real
progress. Congratulations! In the next chapter we're going to attack
a different problem. Hating others. If this is a problem you have,
then let's analyze it together.

Destructive Anger at Others

Let's start by admitting this: **One or more people have probably done things to you that you should hate them for.** For forty years I've listened to teenagers tell me horror stories about what other people have done to them. Every school I visit has teenagers who have been sexually abused for years. Every school I visit has teenagers who have been beaten, some nearly to death, by vicious adults or other teenagers. Every school I visit has countless numbers of teenagers with deep emotional scars from the terrible things other people have done to them.

I've also learned that we suffer not only from truly vicious things, but also from accidental or thoughtless things that others do to us. I've known teenagers who had deep wounds from stupid remarks parents or teachers said only one time to them. I've known other teenagers who were suffering because even though they knew they were loved by their parents, they didn't feel loved deeply enough. I've had teenagers explain what someone did to them, and I couldn't understand how it could have hurt them so badly, but I couldn't deny that it did. I could see the pain in their faces.

Because of experiences like these, I'm not going to tell you that you are imagining your pain. I'm not going to tell you that you have no reason for hating the people you hate. But I **am** going to show you what these feelings do to you and how you can make them less self-destructive.

Start by just telling me what happened to you and who you are angry at. Take your time. Let all the fury out. It could be from one event or countless events. You may hate one or many people. Say everything you want to say. If you're afraid someone else will read this, then use your own notebook paper or just talk out loud.

Dave, I have a lot of anger and pain inside. I need to tell you about _____

_____

_____

_____

_____

_____

_____

_____

_____

_____

_____

_____

_____

_____

_____

_____

_____

_____

_____

Now tell me how you feel.

Right now I feel _____

_____

_____,

because _____

_____

_____.

In the last chapter we talked about the messages on your negative and positive tapes. The bad things that other people have
done to you and the hatred you feel toward them also produce
negative **pictures.** Your negative tape contains not only words you
say over and over to yourself but also pictures you see again and
again.

When you are feeling the pain and hatred you just described,
what images do you see in your mind?

I see _____

_____

_____.

And I see _____

_____

_____.

And I see _____

_____

_____.

Now imagine we made a movie from your negative tape.

You are sitting in a theater and looking up at the screen and all
you see are the terrible pictures you just described and all you hear
are your words full of pain and hatred. Now imagine that you had
to sit in that movie theater from morning until night, for the rest of

your life. However terrible that sounds to you, that is exactly what your life is like **when you are a prisoner of your own hatred and pain.** Other people gave you the raw material for the movie, but you play it over and over again in your head. What they did and said to you once, you repeat a thousand times. What they did to you over and over, you keep alive every miserable day of your life. If you truly hate what happened to you, if it was truly terrible, **then don't keep it going.** If they tried to destroy you, fight back. Don't let them poison your life, your mind, your future.

Believe me, I know how hard it is not to let hatred destroy you. I have talked to thousands and thousands of teenagers who have been through hell. I have heard them cry and scream out their pain. I have shared their rage at the bastards who hurt them. I have seen scars on wrists that have been slashed and slashed again because of their hatred and pain. I have seen the vacant stares of souls destroyed by ruthless people. And I have known more teenagers than I want to count who killed themselves to escape their pain.

If your pain is so great that you have been thinking about suicide, then you must stop reading this book now. Call the toll-free hotline: 1-800-882-3386. Please, listen to me. I have been to the funerals of too many teenagers. Your life is precious and there is no reason for you to suffer alone any longer. Let others help you.

Your struggle may even be more difficult than any I've seen in forty years, but if you've come this far in this book, then there is something in you that wants life, that wants health, that wants to be free of your misery. There is a force, I call it the force of God, in you that is fighting against the darkness and the pain. Take the next step in your struggle and see, as clearly as you can, what your hatred of others is doing to the new life you are trying to find.

Dave, when I look at the new person I am struggling to become I see someone who _____

_____

_____

_____.

     When I look at the hatred and pain I feel, I see this cripples my
new life because _____

_____

_____

_____.

     Go over that again. Why is the hatred, and the pain that comes
from it, awful for you? What do you feel like doing when it comes
over you?

     My hatred destroys my new life because _____

_____

_____.

     What it makes me want to do is _____

_____

_____,

and this is terrible for me because _____

_____

_____.

     I'm asking you to take a big step but I've never known a single
teenager, not one in forty years of counseling, who suffered from
hatred of others who ever found a new life without taking this step.
Stop focusing on the other person and start focusing on yourself.
Forget about the bastard. Let him or her go to hell. **Think about
you.** What can you do to help you get over the grief they've caused
you?

Dave, what I need to do for me is _____

_____

_____

_____.

Keep this going. Tell the bastard off and then tell him or her that you've had it with your suffering. Tell that person what you're going to do for you. Imagine he or she is standing in front of you right now.

I would say to this person _____

_____

_____

_____

_____.

And I'm not going to let you destroy me, because _____

_____

_____

_____.

And I'm sick of the hell you've caused me, because _____

_____

_____

_____.

And what I'm going to do for me is _____

_____

_____

_____

_____

_____.

I'm going to do this for me, because _____

_____

_____

_____

_____.

You're making progress. Go back to some of the things we talked about in the last chapter. Think about the negative tape and the parts of it that contain hatred of others. You've seen that it destroys you, not them. And you know you're sick of the pain that you cause yourself by playing it. Remember that the easiest time to stop this tape is the instant it starts. You've just learned a new technique for stopping it. As soon as you start to see images of people you hate or hear your own hate messages, shut the power off by saying some of the things you just said. Tell yourself you're sick of being sick. Tell yourself what you're going to do for you. Try starting and stopping your own negative tape a few times.

Okay, I'll start by thinking how much I hate _____.

When I hate this person, I say to myself _____

_____

_____.

And the pictures I see are _____

_____

_____.

This makes me feel _____.

But I'm sick of feeling this way! And so I'll tell myself _____

_____

_____

_____.

What I want to do for me is _____

_____

_____

_____,

and I won't let my own hatred poison my new life, because _____

_____

_____

_____.

Try that one more time. Think about someone else who has caused you pain and go through the same steps.

This time I'll think about _____. When I feel angry at this person, I say to myself _____

_____

_____.

And the pictures I see are _____

_____

_____.

This makes me feel _____.

But I'm sick of feeling this way! And so I'll tell myself _____

_____

_____.

What I want to do for me is _____

_____

_____

_____,

and I won't let my own hatred poison my new life, because _____

_____

_____

_____.

Now, best of all, what lessons do you have to teach yourself from our conversation in this chapter?

I must teach myself _____

_____

_____,

because _____

_____

_____.

Here are two stories about teenagers who learned they needed to conquer the hatred they felt for others.

I met Gina in Baltimore. She's about five foot three with a face like an angel. I was using the principal's office for counseling when she came in and told me this story. "My stepbrother is six years older than me. When I was six and he was twelve, he and two of his friends invited me to go to the movies with them. This was kind of strange because they never wanted me to be around. My mother had been married to my stepfather for about a year and I remember she was real happy my stepbrother was taking me to the movies. Probably it seemed to her like he was trying to be a real brother. I think I knew something was wrong as soon as we got around the corner from our house. My stepbrother said we had to go down into this basement 'to wait for everybody else.' I went down with him and he started acting strange. Kind of nervous and too nice. He asked me what my favorite candy was and how I liked school and how he wanted to be 'closer' to me. Then his two friends came down and they said, 'Let's play turn out the lights.' I said I wanted to go to the movies and they said we would, but first we would play a game. They turned out the lights and then somebody grabbed me and first they were tickling me and then they started putting their hands under my clothes. I knew it was wrong and I started crying and then somebody put their hand over my mouth and then they raped me. I don't know how many times. Then after it was over the two boys left and my brother turned on the light. He told me he was very sorry. He said if I told my mom or his father the other two boys would kill him and kill me. He showed me a knife and stabbed and stabbed it into the top of the table. He really got me scared.

"I don't know how much longer it was but I told my mom. She wouldn't believe me. She thought I was making it up. She was afraid of my stepfather. He was a real bastard, he drank all the time and beat her. So she just told me to shut up and 'stop imagining things.' Then my stepbrother somehow found out that I had told my mother. I'm not sure how that happened. Maybe he scared it out of me. He got his friends together and they pulled me back behind our garage. They had some lighter fluid and they set some rags on fire and said they were going to do the same thing to me if I told on them. After that, there was like a pattern of them getting me alone and threatening me and then molesting me. I think this went on for about three years.

"I'm sure my mom knew something was going on but she never stopped it. She finally got a divorce and two years ago we moved to Baltimore. It's when she finally got away from my stepfather that I really began hating her. I always hated my stepbrother and his friends, but it was when I was old enough to understand that my mother should have protected me that I started really hating her. Nobody could ever convince me that she isn't scum of the earth. When I was a freshman in high school I started using marijuana. Then I moved on to coke and pills, downers and uppers. I felt angry all the time, at teachers, at other kids, mostly at my mother. On weekends I'd get so loaded I'd practically be out of my mind. Then one day I went into our garage, closed the door, started the car and tried to kill myself. I woke up in the hospital. My mother came and tried to comfort me but I told her to go to hell.

"They put me in a rehab program. I met a counselor there, a woman named Dianne, and she had been abused when she was little. I must have talked to her for about five hundred hours. She got me to see that all the hatred I felt toward my mother was making me destroy myself. She got me to see that something terrible had happened to me, but I had to choose whether I wanted to let it keep destroying me or not. She told me to hate the pain. She told me to hate all the pain I felt. That might sound weird, but for me it worked. It's like now I still hate my mother, maybe someday I can forgive her, but I put my pain away, in the back of my mind. I don't want to live inside it anymore. I'm sick of being in misery in my own mind."

If you knew this girl what would you say to her?

I would say _____

_____

_____

_____

_____.

What can you learn from her story?

I can see that _____

_____

_____

_____.

Try to apply something from her life to yours.

The similarity between the two of us is _____

_____

_____

_____.

Here is another story you could learn from.

A while ago I was sitting in the airport in Kansas City. I had a layover of about two hours before I could fly home to Newark. A young man came up to me and asked if I was David Toma. He said he had heard me lecture at his high school in St. Louis five years earlier. He was a tall, rangy kid with a letterman's jacket on. His nickname "Spiderman" was stitched on the front. He said he had a story to tell me that he wished I could pass on to other teenagers.

"Both my parents are alcoholics. In the part of St. Louis I grew up in, every neighborhood has a tavern. The big thing on the weekends is for the men in the neighborhood to go down to the tavern and get plastered. All the men have these huge beer guts that hang over their belts. The women don't get drunk that often in public. They do their drinking at home. So every weekend it was the same thing in my house. My dad would go out on Saturday night, my mom would stay home drinking, she wouldn't be doing anything different because she had been drinking all week. And then my dad would come home around dawn and they would scream at each other and break things. Sundays were worse because my brothers and I would tiptoe around the house afraid of waking either of them up. It didn't matter how quiet we were. Even if my parents slept all day, they would get up feeling mean, and usually my brothers or I would get a beating, usually me. I was the oldest and always stuck up for my brothers. I didn't realize it until I moved out but I was afraid all the time, the whole time I was growing up I had this constant fear. All during the week I would be afraid of my mom. Afraid of her and for her. She'd get drunk and fall down the stairs or she'd take too much medication or she'd just scream at me or my brothers and hit us. Then on the weekend it was my mom and dad. When my dad got angry he didn't use a belt, he used a coat hanger or his fists. He beat me plenty of times so bad I couldn't go to school for two or three days. I grew up thinking being scared all the time was normal. Never once in my life did I ever talk, really talk, to either of my parents. I kept myself hid inside myself. It was like I had this secret self inside of me that nobody knew about.

"Then I started getting bigger. I went out for the wrestling team. Every year in high school I moved up two weight divisions. My senior year I was wrestling one sixty-fives and placed second in the city. I had a lot of trophies from wrestling tournaments. Just before Easter I was down in the basement working out, and I could hear my parents screaming upstairs and then my little brother yelling and crying. I went running up the stairs and my dad had my little brother by the hair and I went over to him and he started cussing at me. Then he went to the bedroom to get his coat hanger. When he came out I just stood there and he didn't hit me. Something happened in both of us. He could see something in me. I was shaking, but I was ready to fight back. He just screamed at me and I took my brother downstairs. After that, for about a year I went crazy. I got in fights all the time. I felt like a tough guy. I wanted to just beat the crap out of people. I could tell my dad and mom were afraid of me, but they still beat my brothers when I wasn't there.

"I can't tell you how many nights I lay awake and thought about killing my parents. I killed them in my mind a thousand times. Everything inside me was death. I'd see slasher movies ten times. I gave up wrestling because I didn't like all the training, all I wanted to do was fight. Then I met this girl, Joan, at a dance. She was from the greatest family on earth. When I'd go over to her house I couldn't believe how nice they were to each other. I thought it was all fake, and we had this big fight and she finally convinced me that I was wrong. This made me even angrier at my parents. I went out with Joan for six months and all my rage started coming out at her. The slightest little thing would make me furious. If she was late or if I thought she was looking at another guy, I'd go crazy. Finally one time I slapped her. This was kind of a normal thing to do around my house. She looked at me like I was a maniac. It took me three months to make up to her, and I finally began to see what all the anger I had inside was doing to me. I was growing up to be just like my dad. If something made me mad, I started hitting. I was just pure anger inside and I didn't know how to love. It's not easy to change how you are inside, but Joan helped me. I never tried drugs or alcohol. I was an athlete, I thought I was being pure. I'd seen what beer did to my family. I thought I was totally different. But now I see I was addicted to anger. I loved it. Screaming, fighting, seeing people afraid. Being angry, furious, that was my high. Joan says I should get a tattoo—'like father, like son'—and stare at it every time I want to be crazy. It seems impossible but you can hate somebody so much that you become just like them."

What could you relate to in this boy's story?

His story reminded me of _____

_____

_____

_____.

What lesson could you teach yourself?

I could teach myself that _____

_____

_____

_____.

Try to see some part of yourself in him.

What reminded me most about myself in this boy was _____

_____

_____

_____.

Think of the girl's story and this boy's story and tell me the single most important lesson you can learn about life-destroying hatred.

I have to remember _____

_____

_____

_____.

In both these stories, there was someone else who really helped. The first girl was helped by a counselor, the boy was helped by his girlfriend. I wish I could take you by the hand right now, look into your eyes, and tell you what I have told thousands of others. **Find someone who can help you.** Think of someone right now who you could talk to. Your brother or sister, one of your parents or grandparents, an aunt or uncle. A counselor, someone at church, a youth center, one of your friends. (If there is no one you know, then call one of the numbers in the reference section on page 209.)

The person I should talk to is _____
_____.

Good. Now if you want to, let's talk about depression.

14

Depression

This chapter is not about feeling down or moody or grumpy. When you're in a bad mood or you're grumpy or something is bothering you, it goes away before long. But when you're deeply depressed you feel like you are at the bottom of the world, everything is black inside and out, the depression goes on and on, there seems to be no way out. When you're only feeling unhappy, you can talk to someone else or watch TV or go get some exercise. When you're really depressed there isn't anyone on earth you want to talk to and nothing on earth you want to do.

There is nothing wrong with simply feeling low. Life is full of unhappy experiences. Your mother yells at you, you get a bad grade in math, you lose ten bucks. Roll with the punches, take the bad with the good, feel down for a while and get on with your life. You don't need my advice to get over something that is going to wear off on its own.

But deep depression is something else. You have to fight it with all your strength, because it wants to take your life away. Deep depression and suicidal thoughts go hand in hand. Depression that you don't seem able to escape from is what we'll talk about in this chapter and we'll talk about suicide in the next.

Remember, I said at the beginning of this section about serious teenage problems that I would assume each chapter was about a problem you were experiencing. So, tell me as clearly as you can how you feel when you are deeply depressed.

I feel _____

_____

_____

_____.

Let's find out more about these emotions. What seems to bring them on? First of all, is there a certain time of day when you feel more depressed than others? When are you most likely to be at the very bottom?

The worst time is often _____.

Call that your Darkest Time. We'll come back to it.
Now, when you are depressed, really depressed, what do you do?

When I'm most depressed, what I usually do is _____

_____

_____

_____.

Call those your Dark Actions.
And where do you go when you are really depressed? Your room? Out into the woods? Where?

When I'm really depressed, I usually go to _____

_____.

Call that your Dark Place.
And what thoughts go through your head when you are down and don't see any way out?

What I think is _____

_____

_____

_____.

Call those your Dark Words.
And what pictures do you see in your head?

When I'm really depressed, I often see images of _____

_____

_____

_____.

Call those your Dark Pictures.

Now, can you see how all these things can work together? Dark Actions, Dark Words, Dark Pictures, the Darkest Time, and the Dark Place feed on each other. When you are feeling depressed the worst place on earth for you to go is to your Dark Place. Where could you go instead?

I could go to _____

_____.

And when you begin to think your Dark Words and see your Dark Pictures, your Dark Actions are the worst thing on earth for you to do. They make the depression stronger, deeper, blacker. What could you do instead?

I could _____

_____

or I could _____
or I could _____

_____.

Try this as an exercise. Imagine you know someone exactly like you, your double. Same family, same age, same situation, same everything. Looking at this person is like looking in a mirror. You know this person as well as you know yourself. Then imagine this person comes to you for advice. What would you say?

First of all, I would know this person's Darkest Time of day. When that time approached, I would tell this person to _____ _____.

And I would know what this person's Dark Actions were. Instead of doing those self-destroying things, I would advise this person to _____

_____

_____

_____.

I would give this person good advice, because I know those actions so well! They lead to _____

_____

_____.

One place I would tell this person absolutely to avoid during depression would be _____

_____

_____,

because I know that going there only makes everything worse. Instead of going to that Dark Place, I would tell this person to _____

_____

_____,

because _____

_____

_____.

If this person asked me about their Dark Words and Dark Pictures, I would say _____

_____

_____

_____

_____

_____.

The most important thing for this person to do to stop depression before it began would be _____

_____

_____

_____.

That's a good beginning. What I want you to see in this chapter are the outer and inner ways your own depression works. You do certain things and go certain places and think certain things that feed depression, make it stronger, blacker, and darker. In the first chapter of this book you said you wanted a new life. Now you need to see as clearly as you can the things that feed and strengthen your depression. You thought about the Darkness, now think about the Light.

What things do you think, what pictures do you see in your head, what places do you go to, and what things do you do that strengthen new life in you and lead you toward the Light?

The thoughts that lead me toward the Light are _____

_____

_____

_____.

Places where it is very hard for me to be depressed are _____

_____

_____

_____.

When I'm not depressed at all, the happiest pictures I see in my head are _____

_____

_____

_____.

Things I do that make me feel great are _____

_____

_____

_____.

Let's keep going. As I said before, I never knew a teenager suffering from depression who didn't feel alone. I've heard teenagers say ten thousand times, "I've got nobody to talk to," "Nobody loves me," "I can't reach out to anyone," "I'm all alone." But almost all of these teenagers, when I ask them to think hard, can name someone, a friend, a family member, someone at school they **could** talk to . . . except they don't. They're too depressed to make the effort.

Tell me someone who would be good for you to talk to. Perhaps it is the person you mentioned at the end of the last chapter.

I could talk to _____ and this would be good for me because _____

_____

_____

_____.

Well then, when are you going to talk to this great person?

If I want to keep going on my new life, then I will talk to them

_____

_____.

Here's another suggestion. This may sound a bit strange but I've learned that physical exercise is one of the best cures for depression. It's far easier to be depressed when you're **not** tired than when you are. You can actually be too exhausted to be depressed. Run, work out, do aerobics, or go for long, fast walks. And then go home and try to be depressed. You can't! It takes too much energy. Besides that, you feel good about getting into shape.

Something I could do that would give me real exercise would be _____
_____ .

I would enjoy this because _____
_____
_____ .

Think about what it would be like to be in excellent shape.

I would get up in the morning, and I would feel _____
_____
_____ .

I would look back on how I am now and think _____
_____ .

What kinds of things would you be able to do if you were in really good shape that you can't now?

I could _____
and I could _____ .

Now I get tired if I only _____
_____ .

What would be the easiest thing you could do tomorrow to start getting into excellent shape?

I could _____ .

And then within a week or two I would be able to _____

_____.

In a month or so I could probably _____

_____.

By the end of a year I can see myself _____

_____

_____!

I would feel _____

because _____.

You certainly can't get into shape and beat depression unless
you make some changes in your diet. What you eat affects how you
feel. Medical studies show that there can be a direct relationship
between depression and a poor diet. Eating large amounts of sweets
for example can give you "sugar blues." Tell me what you eat on a
normal day.

A list of what I usually eat on a normal day is _____

_____

_____

_____

_____.

How much junk are you putting into your body? How much
sugar? How much salt and processed food? What advice can you
give yourself about your diet?

The sugary foods I eat too much of are _____

_____.

The salty foods I eat too much of are _____

_____.

My favorite junk food is _____.

The good things I could eat instead would be _____

_____

_____

_____.

The next steps will be to read some letters teenagers have written me about their struggles with depression and then construct your own plan to defeat yours.

Dear Mr. Toma:

I'm 16 years old and a junior at a high school here in Wyoming. I heard you talk about a year ago. I just wanted you to know how much you helped me. My problem is and has been that I am overweight. As long as I can remember kids have made fun of me because of my size. My parents never had too much sympathy because they aren't overweight. They said I lacked "will power," that I was a "pig," that my being fat was my fault. I've been on a hundred diets since the second grade and nothing has worked for long. My whole life it seems like I've either been feeling hungry or guilty for eating. It's a terrible thing to hate the way you look and then have everybody get down on you for something you are doing your best to control but can't. I've never been to a school dance. I almost never dress for P.E. because I hate how I look in shorts. I quit going swimming when I was eight because some boys at our pool laughed at me. If I was crippled, people wouldn't make fun of me, but because I'm fat they think it's all right. Before your talk I had no friends. Every day from morning to night I felt miserable, miserable. I hated going to school because I always felt alone and I hated being home because my mother was always watching my "food intake." I thought all the time about killing myself but I didn't have the nerve.

When you came to our school I thought about not going because I thought you were just going to talk about drugs and alcohol and that wasn't my problem. But I went just to get out of my morning classes. You talked about *everything* and so much of the time it seemed like you were talking right to me! I was crying and I looked around the auditorium and saw all these other kids crying and I had thought they were okay and I was the only miserable one. Then some kids went up to the microphone and began telling about how terrible their lives were and how much they hurt inside. I didn't know what I was doing but I went up on stage and we were all crying together and then you came over and hugged me. That was one of the greatest moments of my life. I went home and thought about everything you said. You made me see that I could destroy my life or save it. You made me see I had the power to do what I wanted. I could take myself down or I could fight back and make myself happy. You said, "Change what you can change in your life and to hell with what other people think." I know now that I *can't* change my weight. I'm a big person, always have been and always will be. *But I can change how I feel inside about that.* And I can change a lot of the things I do. You told us to follow our dreams. I want to help other people like me. I don't know exactly how I'm going to do that but I think I want to go into medicine. Maybe I'll be a doctor someday or a psychologist. It's going to be a hard struggle, but you gave me the inspiration to want to change my life. Thank you so much!

Here's another letter.

Dear Dave:

You asked us to write you letters, so here I am. In the middle of your talk at my school I felt like you were my best friend. Man, you moved me like nobody I ever knew. After you left I never smoked grass again. Here's my story.

On my 13th birthday, that was two years ago, my brother gave me a joint. He said, "Welcome to your teenage years," and showed me how to smoke it. It was terrible, I nearly choked, but I felt excited. I finally got to be like one of the hip kids. By the end of six months, halfway through my freshman year, I was getting high two and three times a day.

Whenever I felt depressed or something bothered me or I felt alone I'd turn to a joint. The more I smoked, the more I wanted to smoke. Weed was like my doctor but it was poisoning me at the same time. When I was depressed, I'd smoke and then I'd feel a little better and then before long I'd feel worse. It took me up a little, mellowed me out and then as it wore off, it threw me even deeper in the hole. Even my brother got a little scared but he couldn't stop me. Nobody could. I was like inside this little prison inside my own mind. I was going down and down and the lower I got, the more I wanted to smoke. In the beginning I used to get high with about three of my friends but then I started doing it by myself so I didn't have to share. Plus that I used to always hassle with these guys. I thought they were stupid and they thought I was stupid, so I thought screw them. I'll do my own thing. I became the most alone kid in the world. I'd just go around school and the house and look miserable but secretly inside I was calling out to people, help me! Talk to me! And then when they would, I would just turn them away. Then my parents found out I was getting high and they went crazy. They had just found out about my brother about two weeks before and then me! They tried to make us enroll in a drug program. My brother got help and I did a little bit. Maybe I was too stubborn, too angry. Then my parents got divorced which depressed me even more but what it really meant was that my mother was too busy feeling bad to pay attention to me. I went back to my old ways. When you came to our school I don't think there had been more than a few days in the whole year when I hadn't been high and that was only because I was broke. I was alone, alone. I only lived for grass. In my head it was like permanent night. You talked about all the kids who had ruined their lives with drugs and alcohol. You talked about the poisons that are in drugs, in grass. It wasn't just one thing you said it was everything all together. I could see down inside myself that I was killing myself. That was it. I knew if I kept being alone I would kill myself. I didn't want to be alone anymore. I went home and talked to my brother, really talked to him and at first I couldn't get through. I told him I was going to quit using and since he didn't smoke as much as me, he didn't want to go along. Finally I bet him ten dollars he couldn't go a week without getting high so he bet me. Then I tried talking to my mother. I tried telling her about my problem but this only made her angry. Then I went to a counselor at high school and she really helped. I'm in a group now of kids like me. We're all former dopers. We meet twice a week. It's tough talking about our problems but I don't feel like I'm living inside total night anymore. You're the one who started me on the right track. I love you.

Here's a letter that came recently.

Dear Dave:

My father died when I was fourteen years old. He was a policeman and one night he was off duty and just sitting on the porch of a friend and a car full of teenagers came by and shot him. We don't know if it was murder or they were trying to shoot someone else. I'm an only child and even though my father and I were never that close, I've had a terrible time getting over his death. Maybe I couldn't get over it because I wished we had been closer and now there's no way we can be. I had nightmares about him dying for a year after his death. My mother and my grandmother tried to help me but as I got older I didn't want their help. I felt like there was nobody who could understand what I was going through. I met this one boy who I thought I was in love with but I was wrong. I wanted someone I could just be myself around but he said I was always too depressing and we would have fights about that and so we broke up. For the last eight months about all I've done is go to school, come home, shut the door and listen to music or just lie in bed and do nothing but feel bad and cry. Even my two best friends have kind of given up on me. They say things like, "Come on snap out of it," and "Just get on with your life." I just can't understand what is happening inside me. I just can't get over the fact that my dad is not around anymore. I am so angry at the teenagers who killed him. Nobody ever found out who they were. I just can't accept that they are living and not thinking anything about what they did. I know I'm just going around in circles inside myself. Being depressed is like a habit I've gotten into. I break out of it every once in a while but then it comes back over me. Writing this letter to you though helps a little bit. I know I've got to do something. This can't be all there is going to be for my life. I don't want to keep going on and on like this so I've got to find some way out. I'm going to keep trying things until I find something that works.

This girl is right—the depression you're feeling now isn't all there is in your future. If you think there is no end to your feelings of misery, though, talk to someone immediately. A good counselor, minister, or therapist can help you find the answers that will work best for you. Being a retired police officer myself, I could especially understand the anger and loss this girl was feeling. But what I told her is that she can't get lost in the hopelessness, because it will eat her up. Maybe one day she will be the prosecutor, judge, or police officer that will help jail the murderers, cop killers, and drug dealers who have invaded our cities and towns.

Now, think about these three letters and all you've written in this and previous chapters. Tell yourself what you need to know about your depression and how you're going to attack it.

I believe that the cause of my depression is _____

_____

_____.

The things I do that add to it are _____

_____

_____.

The thoughts I think that add to it are _____

_____

_____.

When I start to feel depressed, some of the worst things for me to do are _____

_____

_____

_____.

If I want to get better, I have to stop _____

_____

_____,

and I need to start _____

_____

_____.

What I can learn from the stories of the other teenagers is _____

_____

_____

_____

_____

_____

_____.

If I wanted to start a new, happier life tomorrow when I wake up, I should tell myself _____

_____

_____.

Some good things for me to do in the morning would be _____

_____

_____.

What I could do to strengthen my new life in the afternoon would be _____

_____

_____.

If I wanted to keep going on a healthier, happier path in the evening I should _____

_____

_____

_____.

Above all else I must remember this _____

_____

_____.

No book is a magic cure. I said before that you would have to work hard to make progress. If you feel like you're not getting anywhere then you have to do one of two things, go back over sections of this book and spend more time or find someone you can talk to. In other words, help yourself or find someone who can help you.

If you feel like you are moving toward your new life, then go on to the next chapter.

Suicidal Feelings

Here's a letter a mother sent me after her son killed himself.

Dear Mr. Toma:

I hope some of the teenagers you talk to can be helped by learning about what happened to my boy, Terry. He killed himself through a drug overdose two months ago.

I wish you could sit in our living room and look at the pictures of him as a baby. He had the reddest hair! He looked like one of those babies you see on TV. Healthy and happy, cute. I remember taking him to the store and other women and even men would stop me and say I had one of the cutest babies they had ever seen.

Terry and his dad played baseball together from the time he was about seven. His dad started him in the Little League the first year he was eligible. Every night after work his dad would go out in the backyard and teach Terry how to pitch. My son loved baseball. He collected baseball cards and had shoe boxes full of them.

Terry had been in gifted programs all through elementary and junior high. He never set his mind to anything that he didn't do well at. We let him buy an old junk MG sports car when he was 13, and Terry taught himself about engines by taking the whole thing apart and putting it back together. Even his dad was amazed.

I've tried and tried to look back and see what we could have done differently. Terry's dad and I got divorced a few years ago. As nearly as I can tell, Terry took this okay. He spent time with his dad every weekend. They still played ball together. It seemed better for Terry than listening to us fight all the time. But as soon as my son started high school he began to change. He tried out for the school baseball team and didn't make it. He said it was "no big deal." I tried to talk to him about it and he just shrugged it off and then he would get angry when I brought it up.

The high school had "open campus" at noon which meant the kids could go anywhere they wanted as long as they were back by the next period. By the time the school reached me Terry had missed ten afternoon classes. I couldn't believe it. It came out of nowhere. My son had never cut a class in his life.

I sat him down and tried to talk to him but all I could see in him was anger. I had no idea what he was so angry about. I could never figure out where all the anger came from.

Then things started happening fast. All of a sudden it was like a big deal just to be sure he was in school every day. I put him on restriction. I talked to him, I yelled at him, I cried, I begged. His dad got on him, the teachers were after him. When you punish your child as much as you can, take away phone, TV, all his privileges and then he still does what he wants, what can you do? Beat him? Take away food? I had nothing left. He would just climb out the window at nights to be with his friends.

I'm not saying everything was bad. We had times when he would cry and tell me, "Mom, I'm going to change." This would last for a week, once for three weeks. But then he would start missing school again and the whole cycle would start all over. Arguments, restriction, fights, anger, him disappearing. On and on.

Maybe kids will laugh at me but I think his music was part of it. This will really make me sound like a "square." But

I had this wonderful, happy, talented boy and then he starts wearing T-shirts with bleeding skulls on them and listening all day to music that was nonstop rage. The covers of all his albums looked like scenes from hell. Anger. Rage. Blood. No one could ever convince me that the music was good for him. No one could ever convince me that it made him feel better. It doesn't make sense. If I was angry and hurt and lost and then I listened to screaming music full of anger and rage *for hours and hours,* how would that be good for me? What drives me crazy is that you see some of these musicians in court like Ozzy Osbourne and they look all nice and neat and normal and say, "There's nothing bad in my music." Tell me why they don't come to court dressed up like they look on stage? Tell me when they are screaming on stage with whips and black leather that it's all just a joke, just a put-on. Tell me it's healthy for our kids to go to those concerts.

The last picture I have of Terry, I can hardly recognize. He dressed up for Halloween and he looks like Death. It's not a funny picture. He just has all this black makeup on and white circles around his eyes and he looks like he is staring out at you from hell.

I guess I am a totally naive person. I don't know how I was supposed to get "hip." I never raised a child before. Terry was my first and only one. I know now that the whole time he was rebelling he was using drugs. I blame and blame myself for not searching his room. I was "respecting his privacy." I was "treating him like an adult." A week before his 16th birthday my son Terry died from mainlining heroin. Here is the note he left.

"Dear Family and Friends. I've screamed and screamed and screamed and no one heard me. But don't worry. Don't feel guilty. I've got the final solution. Terry."

What is your reaction to this mother's letter?

Reading it I can see _____

_____

_____.

It makes me feel _____

_____

_____.

When I think about Terry, I think _____

_____

_____

_____.

When I think about his mom, I think _____

_____

_____

_____.

More teenagers die from suicide than from cancer, heart failure, or any disease we know of. The odds are good that one or more teenagers in your high school have killed themselves in the last few years. This is the greatest tragedy I face. Boys and girls who never get beyond the beginning of their lives. We will never know what they could have achieved. We will never know how many people they could have helped. They are lost forever.

Please, please listen to me right now. I know what you are going through. I know that you have been full of pain. Feel me reaching out to you. I love you. I have dedicated my life to helping teenagers just like you. This whole book is written just for you, to help you turn your life around. If you don't feel like there is anyone you can talk to, then call 1-800-882-3386, a toll-free hotline. You know if you need help right now.

There is no one on earth worth killing yourself for. Please don't think that you can use suicide to pay someone back, hurt someone because he or she has hurt you. Do you think if you went out to the garage and pounded your thumb with a hammer that anyone else but you is going to feel the pain? If someone else has hurt you so badly that you are thinking about suicide, do you think he or she will really suffer the way you want them to after you're gone. **The only people who will truly hurt are the ones who love you.** A few weeks after you're gone the one who hurt you will think, "Well, that was too bad. I wonder what's on TV." Don't ever hurt yourself to try to pay bastards back. It never, ever works. You are gone and they have the rest of their lives.

Listen to me. You wouldn't go up to someone you love and slap them in the face. But whoever you love would far rather get hit than suffer the agony you will cause them when they die. **Live for the people you love. Don't die for the people you hate.**

I have waited until the middle of this book to talk about suicidal depression. I wanted you to have a good start on your new life. I wanted you to teach yourself lessons about yourself and others, about your past and present and future. I wanted you to see clearly what you do to your mind with self-hatred, hatred of others, and depression.

I wanted you to put your suicidal thoughts into the past. Look back on them. Tell me what they have been like.

Dave, when I felt like killing myself, I felt _____
_____.

When I looked inside, I saw _____
_____.

I hurt because _____
_____.

When I talk to teenagers who are on the verge of suicide, they tell me they see death as "the only solution" to their problem. You've made enough progress in our conversation that you know this is wrong. Tell me why.

When I felt like killing myself, I thought death was the only

solution because _____
_____
_____
_____.

When I look at this now, I see _____

_____

_____.

I want you to think about the part of your personality that you have put behind you. Call it your Suicidal Self. I want you to see this part of your personality for what it truly is, your deadliest enemy. In parts of your past your whole personality has been dominated by your Suicidal Self. Learn to know your enemy.

When I look at my Suicidal Self, I see someone who _____

_____

_____

_____.

What was important to this self was _____

_____

_____

_____

_____.

What this self felt about people who loved me was _____

_____

_____

_____.

Keep going.

Some of the things I did that made my Suicidal Self stronger were _____

_____

_____

_____.

The thoughts I used to dwell on were _____

_____

_____

_____ .

When you really felt like killing yourself, what was your day like?

In the morning I would get up and _____

_____

_____ .

Inside I would feel _____

_____ .

In the afternoon I might _____

_____

_____ .

And inside I would feel _____

_____ .

When I really felt suicidal, in the evening I would probably ___

_____

_____ .

Looking back on how I used to live, I see someone who _____

_____

_____ .

If I knew someone like that I would say, "Listen to me! _____

_____

_____
_____
_____."

Here's a story one teenager told me which might give you more insights on your past. I met this young man before one of my lectures in Cincinnati. He told me he was one of the students in the school who had convinced the administration that I should come lecture.

"I heard about you from my uncle. When you spoke at Fort Ord to his division he wrote me and said I had to get you to come to my high school. I hope you can help other kids like me.

"I'm sixteen and I've tried to kill myself three times. The first time was with a razor and the other two times were with pills. The last time the doctor told me that if the ambulance had gotten me to the hospital ten minutes later, I might not have made it. I took twenty Quaaludes.

"My family life has been terrible. My father is a computer programmer but he uses speed. He says it helps him meet deadlines. My mother is like a secret alcoholic. You almost never see her drinking. She does it in the morning before we get up and late at night. My brother tried to kill himself before he joined the army. In our house it's normal to be crazy.

"I just can't stand to see what my father and mother do to themselves. I've got a druggie for one role model and an alcoholic for the other. Since I've been thirteen I've being doing what I want to. I've tried everything. From beer to vodka, from grass to meth to coke to PCP to every kind of pill. I'm like the school expert on drugs. I've sold the stuff too but I quit a few months ago.

"The first time I tried to kill myself was right after my mom and dad got into this big fight. They were screaming at each other and I was sick of it and so I went into my room and slammed the door real hard. My dad came storming in, yelling at me and then I started yelling at him and he kicked in the speaker on my stereo. Then he told me I was grounded for a month for losing my temper at him! He left and I went into the bathroom, locked the door and got my grandfather's old razor off the top of the medicine cabinet. I tried to cut myself but I couldn't. Then I went back into my room and smoked a few joints. I wanted my dad to come in and catch me but he was upstairs still fighting with my mom. Then when I was pretty high, I put on my ear phones, cranked up the music and it was strange. I looked down at my hands and they were like on their own. I saw myself take the razor and then all of a sudden hack down at my wrist and then there was blood all over. I got scared and tried to stop it. I took a belt and made a tourniquet and the bleeding stopped but there was blood everywhere. I cleaned things up as well as I could with a few old T-shirts and then I stuffed them in the trash. The next morning I put on a long-sleeve shirt so my mom couldn't see the bandages on my wrist and then I went to school really mad because she didn't know I'd tried to kill myself. I told two of my friends and they just said, 'You're weird. Don't get so bent.'

"The second time I tried to kill myself it was really stupid. It was because of a girl. Maybe that wasn't the real reason but that was what brought it on. I had been seeing this girl a little bit since my freshman year and then I met her at a concert and we just started hanging around together more after that. We never actually went on dates. She would come over to my house or I would go over to her house. Then one night when we were both drunk at a party she told me she loved me and I told her I loved her and we went into the back of one of my buddies van and had sex. After that all we did was get high and have sex. We made all these plans about what we were going to do with our future. I was going to open a music store. She was going to be a booking agent for rock concerts. None of this was too realistic because neither of us is good at school. I really got involved with her. The most I had with any girl. We would fight and scream at each other and then make up and get loaded and have sex. Just like my parents, I guess! Then one day out of nowhere she asked me if I wanted to date other girls. I said no. Then she asked me that again another day and said maybe we were getting too serious. Then she said she might want to see other guys and I should see other girls. Then I found out she was seeing this guy who was a drummer. She had been seeing him for about six weeks. So what did I do? I went home and took a bunch of pills just to pay her back! As if she cared! My mother found me and said I was hallucinating about bugs all over me. I don't remember any of this. They took me to the hospital and I had my stomach pumped. I'll never forget lying in bed all alone at night and crying and crying and wishing I was dead.

"The third time I tried to kill myself I can't tell you why. This was three months ago. I feel a lot better now. I don't know why I did it. I had been high off and on for about two weeks. Then one night I was just alone in my room and this guy had given me a bunch of 'ludes to sell and I thought, 'Oh, screw it. Just take them and get it over with.' It was like this evil voice inside me just saying, 'Get it over with. Get it over with.' So I took them and then I woke up in the hospital again. I hope some of what I'm saying you can use to help other people."

What do you feel right now?

I feel _____

_____

_____

_____.

What advice would you give this boy?

I would tell him _____

_____

_____.

What do you see missing in his life?

I see _____

_____

_____

_____.

What should he do about that?

He should _____

_____

_____
_____.

If he keeps taking drugs what do you think his chances are?

I would say_____,
because _____

_____   _____.

You do not have to do drugs or drink alcohol to attempt suicide. I've known many kids as well as adults who attempted or
committed suicide who never drank or did drugs. But if you are
drinking or doing drugs, you are closer than you will ever be when
you are straight to killing yourself. Some drugs like coke, speed,
and crack bring you up, and some drugs like grass, barbiturates,
and alcohol, bring you down. Either way you're going to crash.
Then you start feeling like you're in a hole, you can't get out, you
go farther and farther down. You can't get out of the hole and you
start to feel there is no way out except suicide. Do you know what
I'm talking about?

Dave, _____

_____
_____
_____.

What can you learn about your life from the boy's story and all
that you've said in this part of our conversation?

What I can learn about my own situation is _____

_____
_____.

Just stop for a second now and think how far you've come
since the beginning of this book, even since the beginning of this
chapter. You are fighting for your life and winning. Page by page

you are getting stronger and wiser. **And you get all the credit.** All the healing is coming from you. The words you write in this book are what is turning your life around. Just thumbing through these pages and staring at the empty blanks wouldn't do anything for you. It is your words, the wisdom that comes out of your heart that is healing you. I'm just asking questions. You are filling in the powerful, healing answers. No one on earth could have done for you what you have already done for yourself.

Listen to me! You're fantastic! You are using your own strength and your own insights to create a new future. You are a great person, because no matter what has happened to you, you are not only a survivor, you have also found ways to heal yourself. Someday you will use all you've been through and what you've learned to help others. This chapter really hasn't been about suicide. It has been about your victory over darkness, it has been about your successful fight to conquer everything that has tried to hold you down. You are a fighter. You are wise and strong. You are a beautiful, beautiful person. Do me one favor. Grin right now and feel how much I love you.

It's time for you to put everything you've learned about yourself and your life together. Look back at the progress you've made since the beginning of our conversation. What you have really done is recorded the story of the growth of your new life. Page by page, you have turned away from the Darkness and toward the Light. I want you now to write a letter to yourself. Tell yourself what has happened in our conversation. Go back over each chapter and tell yourself what you learned, what you need to remember, and **the new things you see now that you didn't before.** Just reading over what you have said will teach you lessons that you didn't learn the first time. In your letter to yourself talk about your past, your present, and your future. Talk about the best times you've had and the worst. Talk about the people you love and the people you have hated. Tell yourself what is good for you to think and do and what is bad for you to think and do. Take your time. You will have finished the chapter on suicidal feelings with a beautiful lesson about all that is good and wise in you.

A Letter to Myself About
My Old and New Lives

Dear _____,

Before you started this book you were _____
_____
_____.

I look back at you and see someone who _____
_____
_____.

Your worst characteristics were _____
_____
_____.

Your best characteristics were _____
_____
_____.

Now, I want to tell you chapter by chapter what you have
learned about your old and your new lives. _____
_____
_____
_____
_____
_____
_____
_____

_____

_____

_____

_____

_____

_____

_____

_____

_____

_____

_____

_____

_____

_____

_____

_____

_____

_____

_____

_____.

If you're having a problem with alcohol let's talk about it.

Alcohol

As I told you, I spent twenty-one years as a cop in Newark, New Jersey, one of the most crime-ridden cities in the United States. I've seen horrors I can barely describe—people cut to ribbons after bar fights, women beaten bloody by their husbands, children thrown down stairwells, teenagers hung from rafters, babies raped by their fathers—**and the great majority of all these horrors was caused by alcohol.** I've had guys stab me, shoot me, push me off a fire escape, and the next day tell me they didn't know what they were doing . . . they were drunk. I've seen families wiped out by a lunatic with a gun, senseless killings of schoolchildren by other schoolchildren, faces blasted away because of something that started with a petty argument and alcohol has been the poison behind it all.

There are a lot of myths about alcohol. Few people realize that there is as much alcohol in a bottle of beer as in a mixed drink. Parents who aren't concerned that their kids are out drinking "a few beers" would be very upset if their kids were out throwing down shots of whiskey. But it amounts to the same thing. Every beer you drink will make you as drunk as a shot of whiskey or a Bloody Mary or a screwdriver.

Medical books are full of thousands and thousands of diseases. There are diseases that affect every part of our bodies, diseases for which there is no known cure. Every day on TV we hear about cancer, heart disease, leukemia, brain disorders. But there is no disease known to mankind that kills more teenagers than alcohol. The innocent liquid that you can buy at any corner store and that you see advertised on every other billboard and in every other TV commercial is a poisonous drug. Alcohol can destroy the liver, stomach, esophagus, pancreas, kidneys, lungs, heart, brain, and even nerve endings in your skin. I've talked to countless teenagers who have a strange tingling in their fingers that never goes away. They don't understand it. They ask me, "Dave, what's wrong with me?" I ask them if they are heavy drinkers and every one says yes. Alcohol blocks the body's absorption of vitamin B_{12}, and this vitamin is essential for the proper functioning of the nervous system. The tingling comes from the alcohol they've been drinking, and it could be only the beginning of much more serious medical problems.

We know a million teenage girls a year become pregnant. I've talked to thousands and thousands of girls over the years, and the great majority of them told me they were drinking when they became pregnant. And almost none of them understood what alcohol does to the fetus. There is a well-known medical problem called fetal alcohol syndrome. Pregnant women who drink too much can permanently damage the babies in their wombs. Doctors have documented thousands and thousands of cases of babies born deformed, stunted, mentally retarded, crippled. And what was the cause? The poison of alcohol.

Here is something few people know. Alcohol kills brain cells. Doctors have documented how alcohol causes the red blood cells to clump together and impede circulation of blood to the brain. Red blood cells carry oxygen and when the cells in the brain don't get enough oxygen they die. And once brain cells are gone, **no new ones are ever made.** The brain is the only organ in the body that doesn't replace lost cells. Damage to your brain is permanent. Alcohol can cause brain hemorrhages and can block the small blood vessels in your brain, and if you drink at all, you know what it does to the way your brain works.

Mental institutions, hospitals, and jails are full of people who once thought they were only social drinkers.

The damage alcohol does to lives is all around us. I'm writing this in early May 1991. In the newspaper this morning there is a story about the jockey Willie Shoemaker. He had more wins than any other rider, was world famous, and was admired by everyone as an incredible master of his sport. He had broken just about every bone in his body from falls, faced death numerous times as horses pitched him to the ground, but he survived it all. And now he is fighting for his life, paralyzed from the neck down after an accident in his car. He had been drinking. The greatest jockey who ever lived can't move a muscle in his body because he got behind the wheel when he was drunk.

Alcohol affects your memory, your reasoning, your judgment. Maybe you think I'm going too far. I've asked this question of thousands and thousands of teenagers. **Would you do the same things sober that you do while you're drunk?** I've known teenagers who have set themselves on fire, who have stood up on motorcycles going ninety miles per hour, who have played chicken in their cars, and who have jumped through plate glass windows—and all of them were drinking first.

Tell me the truth. Tell me some of the crazy things you've done while you were drunk. And would you do them while you were sober?

Dave, I remember when _____

_____

_____.

Another time _____

_____

_____.

When I wonder if I would do these same things when I was sober, the obvious answer is _____,

because _____

_____

_____.

You are putting something in your body which makes you crazy. The damage to your body will be irreversible.

Everyone thinks the problem is drinking and driving. That's not the problem at all. Drinking alone can kill you. Teenagers die all the time from alcohol poisoning. Read the papers carefully. Again and again you'll find stories about teenagers drinking and dying suddenly from heart attacks or brain malfunctions and the cause is drinking.

I cannot count the number of people I have known *personally* whom alcohol has killed. I've known cops, schoolteachers, doctors, lawyers, housewives, day laborers, rich and poor, famous and unknown who have literally drunk themselves to death. And all along the way, the lives of all their families, loved ones, and friends have been changed forever. The drunk who is drinking himself or herself to death takes everyone who loves him or her along for the disastrous ride. And what infuriates me is that millions and millions of dollars every year are poured into advertising this poison. Thousands and thousands die or are crippled—physically or psychologically maimed for life—every year by this drug, and advertisers make it look like fun to drink.

Maybe you think you're one of the smart ones. You know all about the dangers of alcohol but think you can handle it. You only get drunk once in a while. Other people get plastered and do crazy things. Not you. You can keep control of yourself. Listen to me, my friend. Hospitals, mental wards, jails, and cemeteries are full of thousands and thousands of people who thought they were just as smart as you. Do you think anybody says, "I know I'm stupid. I'll get drunk and do something that will really ruin my life"? The more confident you are that you can handle alcohol, the more likely you are to have it destroy you. The only way to beat the bottle is to throw it away.

Maybe you think that drinking can somehow make you feel better. Maybe you know all the bad things about alcohol, but you drink because you need to dull your pain. Well, has it helped? Deep down inside you know alcohol is part of the problem, not the cure. You are taking a poison and calling it a medicine. Alcohol is a depressant. You are swallowing large quantities of a depressant to cure depression. That is like trying to cure a migraine by banging your head with a hammer.

*　　*　　*

Listen to a few stories.

"My dad was a very heavy drinker. The whole time I was growing up he'd average about eight to twelve beers a day. That was what was normal. On weekends or at parties there was no counting. It was frightening to go anywhere with him where there was alcohol. We all knew what would happen. He'd start drinking, my mom would always try to stop him, they'd fight, he'd keep drinking, and before long he would be fighting somebody: my mom, one of his friends, a stranger. He broke my mom's nose three times. The older I got the angrier it all made me. My little brothers and sisters were scared all the time. They did lousy in school because they couldn't concentrate. Counselors gave them tests over and over again, but I knew the cause of their learning problems was my dad. Life at home was shit. Every night he'd be drunk and most nights somebody, one of the kids or my mom, would get beat up and every weekend was way worse. I've seen him fight cops on our living-room floor. I've seen him bang my little brother's head against the wall until the back of his head was bloody. He pushed my sister through the door that goes out onto the patio and the next morning he got mad because there was glass all over. He didn't remember anything. That's another thing that killed me. He would be a lunatic at night and the next morning, just walk around like nothing had happened. His big thing was to go get a knife from the kitchen and tell my mom he was going to cut her throat. I can't count the number of times she and all the kids would be locked up in the car with all the kitchen knives on the seat and him banging on the door to get in. Then next morning, there he'd be in the bathroom shaving like everything was normal.

"Now, here's the crazy thing. I spent my whole childhood seeing my dad drink, seeing the terrible things drinking made him do. When I was about twelve I started drinking myself. I hated him and I hated what drinking did, but I didn't think it would do the same thing to me. I had some older friends who drank beer whenever they could steal it from their refrigerator, and they got me to do the same thing. It wasn't hard. My dad was usually so drunk he couldn't keep track of anything. So my friends and I would go out to this bunch of trees in a field and drink a six-pack and throw up and then in a few days we'd drink another. I'd say by the time I was fourteen I was an alcoholic. I never saw the connection between me and my dad until I started going to a youth group for alcoholics. I drank to get away from his drinking and I didn't see my life was as out of control as his. He was the bad guy. I just drank to make me feel better. I just drank to be with my friends. Because I wasn't beating anybody up, I thought what I was doing was okay. What made it not okay was when I started catching my little brother doing the same thing. When I told him to quit or I would beat the crap out of him, he said I was doing the same thing as him, only more. Talking to other kids in my group made me see that if I hated my dad I couldn't let him destroy me and my brother."

What can you relate to in this boy's story?

Dave, _____

_____

_____

_____

_____.

How did you get started drinking?

I started when I was _____,

because _____

_____.

Did you drink alone or with others?

I drank _____, because _____

_____

_____.

What are some of your earliest memories of being drunk?

I remember _____

_____

_____.

I also remember _____

_____

_____.

Another time _____

_____

_____.

Look back at your life when you started drinking. What do you see?

I see a kid who _____

_____.

This kid's world was _____

_____.

This makes me realize _____

_____.

After you started, what were the reasons you kept going? Think hard. Tell me as many reasons as you can. Did your reasons involve your parents, others in your family, your friends, things happening in school, the way you felt inside?

I'll try to give you as many reasons as I can why I kept drinking and then finish with the largest one. Some of the reasons were

_____

_____

_____

_____

_____

_____.

The main reason I kept drinking was _____
_____.

What can you teach yourself right now about drinking?

The best lesson is _____
_____
_____.

This is a great lesson because _____
_____
_____.

Here is another story from a recovering teenage alcoholic.

"I started drinking when I was about seven. My parents always had booze around the house and it was pretty easy to drink and not have them notice anything. I can remember being plastered and playing with my Barbies and puking and then having to sneak into the bathroom and clean it up. My parents never knew what was going on. They were too busy fighting. Mostly it was about money. My dad would scream at my mom about the bills and she would scream at him about the crap he bought and they would go round and round. I think from when I was about ten on I was drunk about every other night of my life. At first it didn't take that much but then it took more. It seems unbelievable now, almost funny, but I had to get jobs baby-sitting to support my drinking. I knew a kid who broke into houses and I would pay him to bring me any of the liquor he found. Of course, I had terrible grades and, of course, this made my parents scream at me, but I knew what the answer was. Vodka. That was my favorite. I could mix it with Pepsi and drink right in front of them. I guess the worse thing that happened to me was when I got my license. That meant I could sneak away to parties and really get blasted. I had a great rep as a drinker. I was like a legend in my own time. Nobody could outdrink me. Then I got pregnant. I used to go to parties and pass out and wake up in strange places and half the time it was with some guy I'd never seen before. I can't honestly say I know who was the father of my baby.

It's weird but I felt so excited to be pregnant. I didn't care about what my parents said. They wanted me to get an abortion. No way. For about the first two months I didn't drink that much but then I started getting depressed as I got bigger. Maybe I saw the reality of what was happening to me. A baby. No father. My parents calling me a whore. No friends. Who wants to hang around with a pregnant sixteen-year-old? I started drinking more. Or I should say I went back to drinking my normal amount.

"But then something weird happened that made me stop. I was in the doctor's office for a checkup and I was crying because I was so miserable. I started praying to God to show me a way to change my life. This will sound really weird but I think He answered me. While I was crying and praying I looked over at the table beside me and there was a pamphlet on drinking and pregnancy. I knew it was wrong to drink when you were pregnant, but there was something about that pamphlet that hit me. Maybe it was God speaking to me. I read it and got really, really scared. The pamphlet talked about how alcohol can affect the fetus, how some babies are born with physical or brain damage. I suddenly began to feel inside myself what I was doing to my child. I was so scared I talked to the doctor. I told him about my drinking. He described in detail how alcohol can cripple the fetus. He put his hand on my stomach and told me what drinking would do to my baby. I walked out of his office crying again, but I knew I'd never take another drink. I don't know what I'm going to do with my life after my baby is born, but I know he isn't going to grow up with a drunk for a mother."

How did this story make you feel?

Right now I feel _____

_____

_____.

What are some of the bad things drinking has done to your relationships?

The truth is _____

_____

_____.

How does being a teenager with an alcohol problem make you feel about yourself?

It makes me feel _____

_____

_____.

What were some of the worst things that happened to you because of alcohol?

I remember once when _____

_____

_____

_____.

Another time _____

_____

_____

_____.

Now, it's time to just let it all come out. Tell me everything about your drinking problem. Tell me about how your drinking relates to things you've talked about in earlier chapters. What has alcohol done to your relationships with your parents?

Dave, the truth is _____

_____

_____

_____

_____

_____.

How has alcohol affected your relationships with your friends?

I must say _____

_____

_____

_____

_____.

Has drinking affected a love relationship?

The truth is _____

_____

_____

_____

_____.

What does alcohol have to do with how you feel about yourself?

Dave, when I drink I _____

_____

_____

_____

_____.

You are doing great. Don't hold anything back. Let all the painful memories come back.

Dave, there are so many things I have inside me. I remember

_____

_____

_____.

And I remember _____

_____

_____.

And I remember _____

_____

_____.

I need to tell you about _____

and about _____.

I'll start with _____ and then go on to

_____ and then tell

you about _____.

Here goes. _____

_____

_____

_____

_____

_____

_____

_____

_____

_____

_____

_____

_____

_____

_____

_____

_____

_____

_____

_____

_____

_____

_____

_____

_____

_____

_____

_____

_____

_____

_____.

What problems were you trying to solve by drinking?

I would have to say _____

_____

_____.

Tell me why drinking is going to keep you from your new life.

Because if I keep drinking, then _____

_____

_____.

I know you understand that you have no chance at a new life if you drink again. I want you to see that very clearly. You have no chance of a new life, no chance of happiness, no chance of realizing your dreams if alcohol is part of your future. Imagine that you return to your old ways. Look into your future and tell me what you see.

If I went back to drinking, I see _____

_____

_____.

In a year or two I will be someone who _____

_____

_____.

Further into the future, I see myself as someone who _____

_____

_____

_____.

Now pick someone you know who is an alcoholic. This disease is so common that everyone knows someone whose life has been ruined by drinking. Tell me about this person.

I am thinking right now about _____. I look at him/her and see _____

_____

_____.

How terribly has this person damaged his or her own life?

The truth is _____

_____

_____

_____.

And how terribly has this person damaged the lives of others?

The truth is _____

_____

_____.

Now force yourself to imagine that you are headed in the same direction. Force yourself to imagine that you will be in the same shape as this alcoholic some day. Maybe in your heart, you know you are already there.

Dave, _____

_____

_____

_____.

The purpose of this chapter has been to tell you some things you may not have known about alcohol and to give you some insight into your own experience with this poison. What have you learned?

I have learned _____

_____

_____.

If you've filled in this chapter with the truth, then you know enough right now to know whether or not you need more help. On pages 209–11 are the addresses and phone numbers of some organizations you can call to find people to talk to. You know whether you have your problem under control or not. The great lesson teenagers have taught me over and over again is that each person truly knows what is best for him or her. You know what is best for you. Your heart is telling you right now what you should do about your drinking.

Right now I am saying to myself _____

_____

_____.

Listen to yourself and you will move one step closer to your new life.

One of the good things you can do for yourself is to keep going in this book. If you also have a drug problem, then let's talk about that next.

Drugs

Some weeks I talk in front of thirty thousand teenagers. I get five thousand or more letters a week and I've been on the lecture trail for forty years. My facts about the damage done to our society by drugs and alcohol don't come from reading journals and studying rats in laboratories; they come from personal contact with hundreds of thousands of America's teenagers.

There are only four ways you can go with drugs. A mental institution. Jail. Death. Or you can quit. I don't care what you're using: acid, meth, pills, crack, coke, ice, pot. If you had seen what I have seen, talked to even a small percentage of the teenagers I have, you'd know you're destroying your life. There is no such thing as doing drugs "recreationally." I know. I've stood beside the graves of too many kids who smoked a little pot, or who did a little coke, or who took a few pills "recreationally." And now they're dead. If you're doing drugs at all, in any amount, you've got a drug problem. You're using drugs because you need to. You rely on them. You can't get by without them. Maybe you want to say right now, "Come on, Dave. I just smoke a few joints. Nothing wrong with that."

Listen to me.

The lies I hear about pot make me sick. It's the "safe" drug. It's "a lot better than alcohol." What "harm can a little joint do"? I'm sorry, but people who say these things don't know what they're talking about. They haven't talked to thousands upon thousands of teenagers, like I have, who have lost their memories, who have gone numb in different parts of their bodies, who have had their reproductive organs ruined, who have brought deformed babies into the world, who have spent years in mental institutions.

Before you light that joint there are 61 poisonous chemicals in it. After you light it, there are instantly 421 chemicals and poisons in that one joint. By the time you take that first hit, you pulled **over 2,000 different chemicals down into your lungs.** Of all the hundreds of poisons you take into your body with each lungful of smoke, none is more insidious than tetrahydrocannabinol. You call it THC. THC is the chemical that gives you the high. If pot didn't have this poison in it, you'd never buy it, as you would not get high.

Not one teenager in a thousand knows the facts about THC. Alcohol is water soluble and so when you drink, it gets flushed out of your system every six to eight hours through urination and sweating. THC is totally different. This poison is fat soluble. When you take it into your lungs it heads for the fatty tissues in your body. Every lungful of smoke you take is storing THC in your heart, your lungs, your liver, your reproductive organs, your brain. One joint will give you a dose strong enough to last from three weeks to four months, sometimes even longer than four months! Even if you smoke only one joint a month, you may **never** be free of the THC poison. And the more you smoke, the more poison is being stored in the fatty tissues in your body. And what does it do? It makes you go numb, it destroys your memory, it destroys your ability to reason, it destroys your will, it destroys your organs.

How do I know? I've had thousands and thousands of teenagers tell me about how **nothing but pot** destroyed their bodies and their minds. I could talk for hours about the horror stories this drug has caused. Teenagers tell me at every school I visit that their memories are going . . . they can't even remember their phone numbers or addresses. I have seen more deformed babies from pot-smoking mothers and fathers than I can count. I have heard the voices of thousands of teenagers say to me, "Dave, Dave, I can't feel anything in my arm . . . my side . . . my face anymore." I have visited thousands of teenagers in mental institutions who had destroyed their minds with pot and will never be sane again.

I have had countless kids ask me what they should do if their boyfriend or girlfriend is using drugs. Here is what I would say to a girl, "I don't care how much you love this guy, you have to go to him and say he must make a choice. Either the drugs go or you go. You must convince him that he can't have you and drugs in his life. If he decides he wants the drugs, *he never wanted you in the first place.* Why would you want someone who has a love affair with drugs? If he can't quit now, don't plan on him quitting after you marry him. He will destroy you and your kids later on. I'd rather see you cry now than suffer for years later. I have told this to thousands upon thousands of kids and many made the right choice and are doing well today. Many didn't listen and had miserable lives, which ended up in nervous breakdowns, divorces, incest, emotional problems, dysfunctional families, unending pain. It's not worth it. Get out now and you will thank me later."

Let me just tell you one story I know very well. The story of my nephew Anthony. Anthony started smoking pot when he was eleven years old. He was a pusher by his early teens. He sold pot to other kids to support his habit. He was arrested 105 times. One day he and two of his buddies went off to get high. Normal day. They'd scored on some really good weed from Mexico. Great stuff. They shared one joint. After a few hits Anthony began to get numb. His arm, his side, and his head began to tingle, and he couldn't feel them. His buddies were sailing and didn't notice anything. He tried to talk to them, tell them something was wrong but they were too stoned to care. After a few hours though they began to get worried. Anthony was acting really weird. Crazed. They took him home and that's when one of my nieces called me.

"Uncle Dave, you gotta get over here! Quick! Anthony's going crazy!" She was crying, in hysterics.

When I got there, the two boys were shaking and scared stiff. My niece was crying. My sister said, "He's up in his room." I didn't hear anything and hoped he'd passed out. The two boys followed me up the stairs.

I opened the door to his room. He'd destroyed everything he could get his hands on. Anthony was huddled down by a smashed window. He turned around, blood poured from a wrist. He looked like living hell. His eyes jerked around and couldn't focus. He wasn't my nephew, there was some crazed monster inside him. I walked toward him with my arms open. I said, "Anthony, you know me. Uncle Dave. What's wrong, man? Let me help you." Suddenly he lunged past me and I grabbed him. He smashed me in the face with his fist. We went down, and it was like wrestling with a madman. Somehow, the two other boys and I got him into the car. He was kicking, screaming, cussing. I managed to get a tourniquet around his arm to stop the bleeding. We got him to the hospital, and he was still fighting and thrashing. The doctors shot him up with tranquilizers and he passed out. I prayed and prayed over him. Finally, after a long time, he woke up. He screamed and his eyes jerked crazily. I looked at him and knew he wasn't going to get better.

For the following five years he spent most of his time in mental institutions. Nobody knows what that one joint did to him. The doctors tell us he'll probably be insane for the rest of his life.

Three boys smoked one joint. Two were okay and one blew his life away. Why? We took the joint down to the lab and had it tested. The chemists told us it was just like the dope kids smoke every day. A normal little pot party destroyed my nephew. I could tell you hundreds of stories just like this one. Smoke pot and you might just as well put a gun to your head. It will destroy you slowly or, like Anthony, it will destroy you quickly.

My nephew's joint was clean. It wasn't laced with anything. But there are hundreds of lethal recipes pushers use to put more kick into their dope. How does this sound? Crush the marijuana leaves and sprinkle a little rat poison on them. Mix it around, add a little roach powder. Maybe spice it up with Drāno or Clorox. Talk to any police chemist. They find this kind of garbage in pot all the time. Why do pushers do this? Make a few more bucks, punch up the dope, experiment with your mind. Maybe you don't believe anybody would do that to your joint? Get serious. Think about angel dust. Angel dust is derived from horse tranquilizers. Smoke a joint laced with this filth, and you would be better off putting a shotgun in your mouth and pulling the trigger.

I remember walking through a cell block with a cop who is a friend of mine. A kid called me over to the bars and whispered, "Hey, call my father. I been in here a few hours and I need help. Call him. Please. Tell him to come down and bail me out."

The cop told me the kid had been in jail for several weeks. He had been a nice, ordinary, middle-class college student. Smoked a few joints once in a while. Nothing too heavy. Then he went to a party and smoked a joint somebody had laced with angel dust.

He went home that night, got a pistol out of his father's bureau and killed both his parents. Then he went into his little sister's room and shot her too.

The poor bastard had no memory of any of this. Angel dust had made him a stone killer, and he was crying behind the bars waiting for his dad to come down and bail him out.

You think he knew what was in the joint he smoked? You think he knew it was going to make him kill his family? Do you think anybody who has their lives ruined by pot ever thinks it's going to happen to them. No! They're just like you **used to be,** right?

Dave, some of the stupid things I used to do on drugs were

_____

_____

_____

_____.

Here's another story to think about. A friend of mine on the police force in Baltimore told me about a kid they picked up. He was wandering the streets naked as a jaybird and out of his mind. They took him back to the station house and locked him up. The kid started screaming and screaming. He screamed for hours. It was driving the desk sergeant crazy. He told one of the cops to go back and do anything he had to and shut the kid up. The cop went back to the cells. The kid stood at the bars screaming and screaming. The cop went over to him. The kid took two fingers on his left hand and clawed his own eyes out.

I know this young man. He is traveling the country right now telling his story to teenagers. What happened to him? He smoked a joint laced with angel dust.

Now maybe at this point you're going to say something to me that I've heard from hundreds of teenagers. Maybe you're going to say that I don't really understand all the pain and pressure in your life. I remember one kid saying, "Dave, I know drugs are wrong, and I know what you're saying is right. But you ain't me. If you had my life, if you had been through what I been through, then you'd see why I'm using and can't quit."

Listen to me. I've been there. I know what it is like to be inside a living hell and to turn to drugs for help.

It started one Sunday when I was a young cop. I got an emergency call on my car radio and headed for the scene. It turned out that the emergency wasn't far from my home. A three-year-old boy was choking on a piece of charcoal. When I got there his mother was screaming and crying. She held her poor kid and didn't know what to do. The boy thrashed, clawed at his mouth, tried to scream. I grabbed him and somehow managed to shake the charcoal loose. It fell on the floor and his mother gasped in relief. But her son didn't move. I was afraid he was dead. I put my mouth over his mouth and began puffing air into his lungs. His little chest rose and fell but his arms and legs didn't move. His mother behind me was crying and shrieking. I blew air over and over into the boy's lungs and begged him to live. I held his limp body in my arms and cried and kept pressing my mouth to his, blowing my air into him. I prayed with all my strength to God to let this poor child live. Then the boy gagged, his arms waved, he jerked, his eyes opened. I ran down the stairs with him in my arms. His mother followed and in a few minutes I handed him to a doctor in the pediatric ward of Newark City Hospital. I paced the halls for an hour. I prayed and tried to comfort his mother. Finally the doctor came out and told me the boy would live. That was one of the happiest moments of my life. I could hardly have been higher. To think that I had saved a boy's life. If it hadn't been for me, that child would have been dead, I told myself. I raced home to tell my wife, Patty. As soon as I burst through the door, I started talking. My kids were all sitting down to dinner. I gave them all a moment-by-moment account of what a wonderful thing their daddy had done. They looked at me with awe and love. I had the incredible joy of being a hero to my own children. Then, my five-year-old son, David, Jr., began to choke and couldn't get his breath. I slapped him on the back. He coughed. Nothing happened. He began to go red, crying and gagging. I grabbed him and began to shake him. The kids started screaming. Patty grabbed me. My boy was choking to death in my arms. I shook and shook him. The kids screamed, "Daddy, you're killing David." I went crazy, shaking David, yelling at him, pounding him on the back. Patty tried to yank me away. I screamed at David to cough. A neighbor came in and called emergency. That's what I should have done right away. I had my son upside down, shaking him. Before I knew it, the ambulance was there. I was out of my mind with fear. They took my son from me. I ran for the car and sped behind the ambulance all the way to the hospital, the same one I had been at hours before with the other child. The same doctors worked on my boy. Nobody could keep me out of the operating room. I can see my son right now, lying on the table, the doctors crowded around him. They gave him a tracheotomy. They did their best, but finally one of them turned to me and just shook his head. I screamed, I couldn't believe it. I found myself in Patty's arms, we were crying and sobbing. I hated God with all my heart. How on earth could He have played such a hideous joke. On the same day I save one boy from choking to death, my own son chokes to death in my arms.

Over the following days we all fell apart. A neighbor came by and was cruel enough to wonder what would have happened if I had called emergency immediately. But she was right. I had lost my head and perhaps cost David his life. Me. The big-shot cop had totally blown it. Over the next week, I began to go way down. Patty was half-crazy, but she had to hang on because I couldn't. My children would ask when David was coming home. I thought about him night and day. I relived the night he had died a thousand times. The look on his face as he choked. The terror in his eyes as I screamed at him and banged on his back. The way his limp body felt in my arms just before the paramedics pulled him away.

Day after day I was crazy with rage and grief. I screamed at everyone who tried to help. Just when my family needed me the most I let them all down. Patty begged me to get help. Finally I listened to her. I saw a doctor who prescribed some tranquilizers. He said I needed to "calm down." Smart guy.

In a few months it was Christmas. The first Christmas without my boy. I wandered the streets in a daze. I felt like my soul had been turned inside out. I remember seeing a little telescope in a shop window my son had wanted. Like a crazy man, I went in and bought it for my dead boy. I stumbled outside, weeping, I could hardly walk. I had the toy and no son to give it to. I walked for two blocks weeping as the Christmas crowds poured past me. I wanted someone to say something to me so I could smash them in the face. I didn't know where I was, where I was going. Then all of a sudden I was tearing open the bag. I had the box in my hands, I ripped it open and smashed the telescope against the wall. I wanted to smash my whole life to pieces but I didn't know how. Then I put my hand in my coat pocket and felt the little bottle of pills.

Over the next few weeks I began popping more and more. The drugs were just what I wanted. What I wanted was something that would take away the pain and that would destroy me at the same time. I began doubling and tripling my dose. I didn't have to go back to the doctor for a prescription. The streets of Newark were my pharmacy. Before long I was up to a hundred tranquilizers a day. At home, at work I was a doped-out zombie.

Then one day I saw some cops from my precinct coming up the front walk. I begged Patty to tell them I wasn't home. Running toward the kitchen in the back of my house, I knew my career was over. Guys at work knew I was a doper and now had told the brass. Here I was, the cop with the incredible conviction rate, shaking like a real junky, scared to death of a knock on the door. I begged and pleaded with God to save me. Finally Patty found me and told me she had convinced the men I wasn't there and that I would get straightened out. I looked at her and we both cried. We knew there was no solution. I cried in my wife's arms like a baby and wondered where I could get some more pills.

Then my nephew Ronnie came in. I had busted this poor kid plenty for his heroin habit. He looked at me sobbing and he knew exactly what was wrong. "Hey, Uncle Dave," he said grinning. "What's the difference between you and me now? You're strung out on your junk and I'm strung out on mine." I had no answer for him. He was right. Patty left the room. I don't blame her for being sick of me. I turned to Ronnie and begged for help. He should have spit in my face. He put his hand on my shoulder and said, "Tell me about it. I know what you're going through." Something broke loose inside me and I began telling him about my grief and pain. I talked for hours and he just listened and looked at me with incredible love and understanding. Those hours were the beginning of my long road back.

I vowed someday I would do for others what my nephew Ronnie did for me. I'm no psychologist. I'm no minister. I've got no magic answers. I'm just someone like you who knows what hell is like. No matter who you are, no matter where you are when you are reading this, I pray to God that you can feel me reaching out to you right now. Know that I love you. Know that I understand.

With all my heart I hope you're not one of those people who thinks they can handle drugs, who uses drugs and thinks they aren't addicted. Listen to me. Let me explain what an addiction is.

One of the big problems in our society is that we hear about addictions on TV, in books, in the print media, and in lectures, and unfortunately, most people—including professionals—don't understand addiction. What you don't understand, you can't teach. Let's just take marijuana as an example. Let's say you smoke pot one time and you like the feeling. You go back a second time. It doesn't matter whether the second time is the next day or ten months later, you went back because you liked how it made you feel. You were looking to get that feeling you got earlier. So anytime you are feeling down, lose a job, fight with your family, or are thinking nothing is going right in your life you will smoke pot again because of what you think it will do for you. It doesn't matter how often you smoke. If you go back, **you have an addiction.** Always remember 95 percent of an addiction is in the head and not the body. One of my nephews went to many rehabs and was detoxed many times. Why did he go back to drugs after being clean for one or two years? His body didn't need it, his mind needed it. That's what an addiction is all about. So if you're doing it at all, get one thing straight, you're hooked. If you check the dictionary it says that an addiction is "being given over to a pursuit, practice, or habit." In terms everyone can understand, you have become a slave to the drug you are using. It controls you. You don't control it. Again. No matter how little or often you use drugs. If you use them at all, you've got an addiction.

In your heart, you know what I'm saying is true. Talk to me.

Dave, I have so much I need to say. I _____

_____

_____

_____

_____

_____

_____

_____

_____

_____

_____

_____

_____

_____

_____

_____

_____

_____

_____

_____

_____

_____

_____

_____

_____

_____

_____

_____

_____
_____.

Now, let's look at your addiction in more detail. How old were you when you first got started with drugs?

I was about _____ years old.

What made you start?

I guess I started because _____
_____
_____.

How did using make you feel when you first started?

I felt _____
_____
_____.

What made you keep going?

I kept using because _____
_____
_____.

When you first started using drugs what was happening in your family at the time?

A normal day in my family then was _____
_____
_____
_____.

When I look back at my family life, I see _____

_____

_____

_____ .

What was the connection with your drug use?

I would have to say _____

_____

_____

_____ .

What can you teach yourself right now about the start of your addiction?

I can see _____

_____

_____

_____ .

What drugs have you used and what have they done to you?

Well, Dave, I have used _____

_____

_____

_____

_____

_____

_____

_____ .

Most teenagers who use drugs go through different stages. Sometimes they go back and forth between heavy drug use and light drug use or they start light and just go deeper and deeper into drugs or they start with one drug and go on to others. Think about your whole experience with drugs. What stages have you gone through?

Right now I am thinking about when _____
_____
_____
_____. Another stage was when _____
_____
_____
_____.

Another stage I went through was when _____
_____
_____
_____.

Now I'll just try to put the stages in order by starting with the first: _____
_____
_____
_____
_____
_____
_____
_____
_____
_____
_____
_____.

There is a chance that you're thinking right now that you have been so deeply involved in drugs that there's no way you can be helped. I've had countless cases that seemed like there was no hope, kids who were doing every drug imaginable and today most of them are clean and doing well. Let me give you just one story out of many.

Four weeks ago, a friend of mine called me about his friend's daughter who needed help badly because she had a very serious drug problem. Half an hour later I was sitting in a restaurant with this girl, call her Mary, and the friend who had called me. Mary's legs were black from drug-induced bruises, both her arms were covered with heroin tracks, I could see seeping sores along her collar bone and I later learned these sores had maggots. She looked like she had been dug up out of a grave. She had lived for eight years on the streets of Harlem and was doing every drug imaginable, some of which could kill a nonuser instantly. She only came to me because my friend dragged her. She said she was twenty-nine and had been doing drugs since she was twelve. She was convinced no one could help her and was ready to die. Just about every hospital refused to admit her because of her terrible condition and because she was on a high dosage of methadone. Methadone is one of the toughest drugs to kick because it gets into the cells and bones of the body.

I called two friends of mine, Dr. Joseph Maudi and Dr. Tony Acampora, at Union Memorial Hospital in Union, New Jersey. They and I worked with Mary for ten days, ten days of excruciating pain and horror for her. I taught her how to go with the pain and gave her all the love and strength I could. I then placed Mary in one of the best rehabilitation centers in the country. After twenty-one days there, she is a completely different person. Free of drugs, she is talking rationally, and has learned about God, love, her feelings, and the source of the pain in her life. She has made a transition that's hard to believe. She taught me again what I have learned many times in my career. **There is no such thing as a hopeless case of addiction.** I don't care if your friends have given up on you. I don't care if your parents have given up on you. I don't care if you've been doing drugs for twenty years. I have seen people who were standing at death's door who have fought back and found a way to turn their lives around.

Now, my friend, do what you've been doing all through this

book. Teach yourself the lesson you really need to learn at this important time in your life. What do you need to learn about drugs?

I must never forget that _____

_____

_____.

And when I start to forget this lesson, what I will do is _____

_____

_____.

One more question. Next time you think about using, what is the strongest, most forceful thing you can say to yourself?

Next time I feel like starting, I'm going to tell myself _____

_____

_____.

I believe this will work, because _____

_____

_____.

This whole book has been about your progress in building a new life. By this point in our conversation, your old life is behind you. You are thinking in new ways. You have insights into who you are and what your world is like. You know what builds new life in you and what weakens it. Therefore, you know if you have your drug problem under control or not. The whole purpose of our conversation is for you to learn what you need to know in order to guide your own life. If you need help, then contact someone (see pages 209–11). If you are suffering from the last problem we'll deal with, involvement with Satanism, then let's talk about it.

Satanism

In every school I go to these days I ask this question, "How many of you kids know someone or have heard of someone involved in Satanic practices?" On average **one-third** of the students raise their hands! In the last few years alone, I have talked in hundreds of elementary, junior high, and high schools all across our country and have heard innumerable stories about young people participating in devil worship. I have had more kids than I can count, including elementary school kids, confide to me that they drink the blood of dead animals. It's a shame that Geraldo Rivera and others in the media have covered Satanism in such a sensationalistic way. When I tell adults, "Satanism is on the rise in our country," they look at me like I am crazy. But the kids I talk to know the truth. The kids can tell me the names of bands who play devil-worshiping music, they can recite lyrics that are full of hate-filled Satanic messages, they can name friends, and when they're honest sometimes even themselves, who have been to "devil churches."

Society has to wake up to the evil menace of Satanism. The more we ignore it, the more we run away from it, the bigger it will become. Listen to me. Throw those damn Ouija boards away. Stop fantasizing about miracles with spirits. You cannot serve two masters. You either serve God or Satan. If you want to be miserable, depressed, see evil visions, and think about suicide, then pick

Satan. If you want to be happy, lead a productive life, and help the world be a better place, then pick God.

Here are some stories I've heard from just **one** school I visited early this year. This high school is in the Midwest, in the center of a hardworking, middle-class neighborhood. Every year they produce one of the finest football teams in the area. This school has some of the finest athletic facilities I've seen; their library is large and well staffed; the administrators are top notch, dedicated, innovative. The teachers I talked to were enthusiastic, creative, and student oriented. They are supported by one of the largest, most energetic PTAs I have ever seen. And in this wonderful school, there were hundreds of kids who had experiences with Satanism. It's not any different from many, many schools I have visited in the last few years.

My first day I talked to the entire freshman and sophomore classes, about fifteen hundred students. Toward the end of my lecture I asked for a show of hands of how many knew someone involved with Satanism. About a third of the teenagers in the auditorium raised their arms. Many of the teachers and administrators were sitting in the front row. I looked down at their shocked faces and asked them if they were aware of this problem. They all sadly shook their heads. Of course, they weren't aware, and *it was right under their noses.* They had never brought the subject up. Talking about Satanism makes you sound like a weirdo, a nut case. After my lecture, here are some of the first stories I heard teenagers tell me.

"I lived next door to this woman whose husband left her with a baby. She was usually stoned but seemed pretty mellow. She was always nice to me. We used to smoke weed together sometimes. She knew some bikers and she knew I liked motorcycles, so she asked me if I wanted to go to a 'meeting.' I said sure. We went down to this place next to a bar and there were a lot of bikes outside. Inside there was loud heavy metal and I thought, 'Hey, great, a party.' I went in and it was really weird. There was a bunch of chairs and a guy up in front in a black robe and he was talking to a bunch of people about something. The woman took me into another room and said I had to take off my clothes and put on a black robe if I wanted to go into the meeting in the back room. This didn't seem that cool, but she said it was going to be great and I could have all the drugs I wanted, uppers, downers, weed, crack, coke, everything was free at the meeting. She said, 'Just put the robe on over your clothes and maybe nobody will notice.' I did. She stepped into a little room and came out with her robe on. I felt pretty weird but I followed her into the room the music was coming from. Everybody was in the center of the room dancing around some candles on the floor. She went over and started dancing and spinning around.

"A guy came up to me and said I was in a new kind of church. He told me they worshiped Satan and asked me what kind of drugs I liked. He gave me some pretty good dope to smoke and we sat down in a corner and he told me that I should join. It was like having a party with the devil. He explained that the devil was really good, that he wanted people to have pleasure and not feel guilty. The whole idea of the church was to do away with guilt. He said worshiping the devil meant doing away with inhibitions. That sounded good to me.

"I started going to these meetings with the woman. Mostly it was just getting high and dancing and saying weird things in some foreign language. About the third time I was there I found out there was another room where they killed animals. They said that anyone who told 'outsiders' about the church would be killed. This seemed pretty weird to me at the time because it didn't seem that hard to find out anything you wanted to. It had been easy for me to join.

"Then the woman started taking her baby to the church and leaving the baby in another room. I didn't like that very much but I thought, well she's the mother. She wouldn't let anything happen to her own kid. I must say she treated her baby pretty poorly. She was always yelling at the baby and complaining about all the mess he made.

"One night we left and she didn't have her baby with her. I asked her and she said, 'Oh, a friend in the church is having him over for the night.' A week later she still didn't have the baby and I asked her about him, and she said the baby was visiting another friend of hers. She was acting really weird and nervous and when I said she must be missing her child she got really mad. She started cussing me out and so I just left.

"I went down to the church by myself the next week and it was closed up. Then the lady just kind of disappeared. She didn't move away. All her stuff was still there, even her car. The landlord came by and asked me if I knew anything about her and I said I didn't. Then the police came by and asked me if I knew anything about the church. Some people they had talked to had given them my name. I told them I'd been there a few times and didn't know much about it. They said they had found a hole in the backyard with the bones of children in it. Then I told them everything I knew about the woman and her baby and I never heard any more from them. Then someone burned down the church. I wish it had been me."

For the last several years I have been trying to wake people up to the massive problem of Satanism. I can hardly express to you the enormous threat Satanic groups pose—under their influence, many kids have already maimed or killed themselves, their parents, a friend, or a family member. Many others are contemplating doing it.

Almost all of the kids who have become involved in these groups are also abusing alcohol and other drugs. These kids have what I call a "spiritual disease," and they need help to develop a positive higher power and self-image to counter the horrible negative powers at work in these groups. Alcoholics Anonymous and Narcotics Anonymous can be very effective in providing the kind of good spiritual influence these kids need. But please, if you or someone you know has become involved with one of these groups, and if they have attempted to influence you or your friends in any way to do damage to yourself or anyone else—call the police, tell your school's guidance counselor or any adult you trust, and, whatever you do, stay away from them. For more help and information, please see the listing for the Cult Awareness Network on page 210.

Here is another story a teenager told me.

"Where I used to live, right down the road from us was a church that worshiped the devil. I went there once or twice but my friends went there a lot. One of the things the people in the church did was round up stray cats and bring them to their services. First they would hang the cats from ropes and then torture them. They would cut off their tails, their legs, and then skin them. The second time I was there I saw this. The idea was that the more evil you did the more the devil would reward you.

"My friends who went there a lot were also heavily into dope, mostly crack. The man who ran the church said that drugs 'helped liberate the spirit.' Whatever you wanted to do was okay. Drugs, sex, alcohol, stealing, all these were things that the devil loved, and the more you did them the more 'earthly rewards' he would give you.

"I have nightmares I can't get over. I can't stop thinking about something. My friends took one of my other friends to the church. They got him loaded. Then they tied him up and cut both his legs off. I don't know why they did this. They were put in prison."

As this boy told me the end of his story he was sobbing.

Here is another story I heard the same afternoon.

"My oldest sister is involved with Satanism because of her boyfriend, Davey. I never knew this until I went to live with her after my parents broke up. Everything looks normal in their apartment except when you go into their bedroom they have all these creepy pictures of the devil and black candles and over their bed is a big crucifix hanging upside down. At first I just thought they were kind of playing around with this stuff. I just thought the music they listened to really sucked and that was all. It was all this kill, kill, kill, hate, hate, hate stuff. Davey has been in jail a few times and is pretty crazy. He has a thing about snakes, he's got snake tattoos all over his arms.

"One day I came home and the music was going really loud and I went into the bedroom looking for them and he was in there with the black candles in a circle on the floor, feeding a rat to his boa constrictor. He was kind of laughing and it made me sick. I told my sister I thought he was crazy, and she said I shouldn't judge people! Then they started having parties, and it got really weird. Some of the people who came over were like old hippies from the sixties who were stoned all the time and used to talk about black magic.

"One night they had some kind of ceremony and killed a chicken and rubbed the blood on themselves. That's when I tried to leave. I ran away for three days but I couldn't survive on the streets. I was broke, I slept in the basement of an abandoned building. My father had left the state, and my mother was shacked up with some guy and was angry at me cause I had gone to live with my sister. She said, 'You made your bed, now sleep in it.' I had nowhere else to go, so I finally went back to my sister's and I tried to talk her out of what she was doing.

"She said I didn't know anything about the 'Black Arts.' She said that a person could have incredible power if they would give up their soul to the devil. She said she knew people who were rich because they knew how to practice the Black Arts and she wanted to learn too. She said if I was going to live there, I would have to abide by her beliefs and rules. She said to look at how screwed up my life was, what did I have to lose? She kept arguing and arguing with me and we were drinking and I got pretty loaded so finally I said okay. I was so depressed I didn't think I had anything to lose.

"That night they had another party. It was worse than any of the others. All these weird people came over and they were all so excited that I was going to join their group. They put out all the lights and lit black candles all over and everybody got really stoned. Then this old woman came in with this black robe on, and my sister said she was a priestess of the Black Arts. Davey brought out his snake and everybody began dancing around with the snake and getting more and more loaded. The old woman said it was time for a sacrifice and they all started howling and screaming. They brought out a bunch of rats in a washtub and everybody crowded around and then Davey put the snake in. The snake wouldn't eat, and Davey was so loaded he went kind of crazy. He took the washtub and ran out to the back and then when he ran back in the snake was in pieces. The people picked up the pieces and began dancing and screaming. I ran. I didn't know where I was going or what was going to happen to me and I didn't care. I just wanted a car to hit me or something. Some cops found me and I told them what had happened at my sister's and one of the cops was incredible. He took me over to his aunt's house. She was so nice. I don't know how she could have been, I was half-crazy. Then the cops went back and busted the party for drugs, and I heard my sister and her boyfriend made bail but that's all I know about them. I'm living in an apartment above the aunt's garage. I pray for my sister every night, but I won't see her or talk to her for a long time."

If you have been involved in Satanism, now is the time to empty your heart of horrors.

Dave, I have to tell you about _____
_____
_____
_____
_____
_____
_____
_____
_____
_____
_____
_____
_____
_____
_____
_____
_____
_____
_____ .

It's important for you to think hard and clearly now. What were your first experiences? Why did you get involved?

At first it seemed _____
_____
_____
_____ .

What happened was _____

_____

_____

_____.

I think why I got involved was _____

_____

_____

_____.

What were some other things that happened to you?

I remember _____

_____

_____

_____

_____

_____

_____.

What was missing in your life?

What I was looking for was _____

_____

_____

_____.

If you look back through this whole section on serious teenage problems, you'll see that we have talked about some devastating experiences. You've listened as other teenagers have talked about self-hatred and hatred of others, depression, suicide, drug and alcohol addiction and now, in this chapter, Satanism. Throughout our entire conversation, I've been asking you to see your life more clearly, teach yourself what you need to know, learn from others, and take my advice whenever it made sense to you.

At the start of our conversation, I asked you to make a decision about finding a new life. Then, I told you toward the end of our talk, that I'd ask you to make one more decision. If you have come this far and if you have been involved in Satanism or any of the other problems we have discussed, you know enough to make your second decision. In a few moments, I'm going to ask you to decide whether or not you can solve your problems without God's help. But first let me tell you about my experience and give you some advice.

I've spent my whole adult life dealing with young people in crisis. I've seen some succeed and some fail. All the success stories have two things in common. First, I've never known a single teen-ager who conquered their drug or alcohol addiction or who over-came other serious problems alone. Unfortunately, there is no way in this book that I can take you by the hand, as I often do for teens I talk to, and lead you to a good counselor or put your hand in the hand of a close friend of yours. You're going to have to take that step by yourself, and I urge you to do so. You picked up this book because you wanted a new life. You've worked hard seeing yourself more clearly and talking about your problems. I hope by now you've found at least one other person to talk to besides me. If you haven't, a good way to start would be to find someone with whom you can share a little of what you've written in this book. As I say, I've never known a teenager who beat his or her problems without the help of another person. Second, I've never known a teenager, or anyone else, who has conquered his or her problems without a relationship with God. Maybe the word *God*, perhaps because of your experience with hypocritical religious people, has a negative connotation for you. Perhaps you grew up in an oppressive reli-gious atmosphere or have had very harmful experiences with mem-bers of a church. I have, for example, counseled teenagers who were molested by members of the clergy. If the word *God* is associated with strong negative feelings, then whenever I talk about God, simply think of a "Higher Power." But try to remember this: God is not the one who hurt you. God is the force of love. If you have to, be angry at those who twisted His message, but don't let your anger keep you from experiencing His healing power.

I am convinced that you have to find the spiritual force far greater than yourself to find true inner peace and strength. If you could only spend a few days with me as I listen to teenagers tell their stories and hear from the ones who have been victorious, you would be convinced I am right. The faces of the ones who have found God shine with strength. Their old lives are gone. They are living their new lives through God's power.

Your first decision was to look for a new life. Your second decision is whether or not to ask God into this new life. If you have been involved with Satanism I think it is especially important for you to seek God's help. You must make a decision for Him now. You need His holy power and His healing love. I don't think you have any hope without Him, but whether or not you go on to the next section is up to you.

Dave, my decision is _____

_____,

because _____

_____

_____.

If you're ready to let God help you solve your problems, then you are truly ready for your new life. Turn to the next section and I'll help you see your spiritual life more clearly.

Part 3

You and God

19

Your Relationship with God

Let's start by talking about some of the negative feelings you might have about God. Teenagers I've talked to who were turned off to the spiritual life were either angry because they felt God had done something wrong or angry because some religious person or group had hurt them.

If anyone who claimed to believe in God has harmed you, then know that they were not acting from God's will. Be angry if you want to at these people, but don't blame God for the actions of fools. No true religion teaches that it is God's will that innocent people should be hurt. If some adult has used religion to make you feel terrible, then be angry at that adult, not at religion. Be angry at this person for perverting God's love. But don't let him or her keep you from your own spiritual life. Don't turn away from God, because He is the one who always helps you. Don't let a terrible person keep you from the great gifts of life, the gifts you find when you turn toward God's light.

Perhaps you are angry at God. Maybe something terrible has happened in your life and you are angry at Him for causing it to happen. For example, perhaps someone you love died or was seriously injured and you believe God is to blame. I have no easy answer for you. People have written millions of words starting with the book of Job centuries ago about the bad things that happen in human lives. All I can do is tell you about my own experience. When my son David died, I was furious not only with myself but also with God. I cried out in rage at Him. How could He let something like this happen? I blamed Him with all my heart. And my anger drove me down and down. My fury at God drove me into darkness and I found nothing but suffering. And I did nothing but cause suffering to all those around me. But then I began to talk to my nephew Ronnie, the drug addict who I had busted countless times. He had every reason on earth to hate me and he showed me love and compassion. Little by little my life turned around and little by little I began to turn to God for strength. This is what I learned. When terrible things happen we can do one of two things in our spiritual lives: We can either rage at God—and this leads to living hell—or we can turn to Him for strength—and this leads to healing. Some people tell me that when they have turned to God they have found answers. They see that the terrible event had some purpose in God's plan. Other people tell me that when they turned to God, they found no answer but they found the strength to keep living. My own spiritual life has taught this: Turning away from God in a time of great trial leads to incredible misery; turning toward Him leads to the incredible healing. If something terrible has happened in your life and you want even more misery, then hate God in your heart. If you want healing, then open your heart to Him and feel His strength.

Think back. You have known good people who believed in God. Who were they?

The best people I've known who believed in God were _____

_____

_____.

Pick the one you admire the most and describe this person.

I'll pick _____. When I think of this person, I remember

_____

_____.

This person was the kind of person who _____
_____
_____.

Now, tell me about the most loving person you ever knew.

Some of the most loving people I knew were _____
_____
_____.

Perhaps the most loving was _____, because
_____
_____.

Tell me some more loving things this person did.

I remember when _____
_____,
and I remember when _____
_____.

Now, can you see God's spirit within this loving person?

The truth is _____
_____.

Remember this person; in a few moments you may want to talk more about him or her.

For now, let's think more about your contact with God's spirit. I believe every person has many contacts with Him and that all we need to do is look back carefully through our past. When have you felt closest to God? I want you to think back through your past and remember any events that seemed to be miracles. Or perhaps times when you were in church and you felt God's presence. Think about other people, besides the ones you talked about above, who seemed to be full of His spirit. Or perhaps you saw an incredible sunset or stood beside the sea or in a field of flowers and felt close to God. When have you felt closest to Him?

You think for a while letting the memories return.

You think about _____
_____
_____.

And you think about _____
_____
_____.

You remember when _____
_____
_____.

And then you say,

Dave, when I ask myself when I have felt closest to God, I must say _____
_____
_____
_____
_____
_____
_____.

Now think about the times when you felt His hand on your life. When you did feel God guiding you or talking to you? When did He save you from doing something wrong or lead you toward something right?

When I think about the ways God has guided my life I remember _____

_____

_____

_____

_____

_____

_____

_____

_____

_____.

Now pick one person from your entire life who seemed to you most full of God's spirit. It could be someone you mentioned above or who you've read about or seen on TV or in a movie. This special person is full of love and may even seem holy to you. More than anyone else you know or have heard about, this person is truly good. Look deeply into this person and you will see God's spirit.

You pause and think of several good people.

The ones who come to mind are _____

_____

_____.

If I had to pick one person who seemed most full of God's spirit I would pick _____

_____.

Why?

Because _____

_____

_____.

Tell me more.

When I look at this person, I see _____

_____

_____

_____.

What are some of the things this person did that seemed full of God's spirit?

I would say _____

_____

_____

_____.

What kind of advice would this person give you about your life?

This person would tell me to _____

_____

_____,

because if I don't, then _____

_____

but if I do, then _____

_____.

Now here is a very important question. Tell me two things you could do right away that would make you more like this person you admire.

I could stop _____

_____.

And I could start _____

Here are two stories from a single family I know, which might help you see God's presence in your life more clearly.

"It's hard for me to describe my mother to anyone who didn't know her. Her whole life was centered on her family. When I was little I can remember my dad being a very vicious man. He was extremely jealous. If he and my mother went out dancing or something and he thought my mother was even looking toward another man, he would go crazy when they got home. He would yell and scream and break furniture. Finally one night she couldn't take it anymore. She came into the room where we were sleeping and told us to get our things together, we were moving out. We lived in our car for two weeks.

"She had almost no education and was too proud to accept charity. She worked twelve and fourteen hours a day just to feed us all and finally got enough money together to rent a place. I never knew anyone who worked harder. She went to school, got her G.E.D. and after fourteen years of going to college part-time got her B.A. Through it all, her faith in God gave her the strength she needed to keep going. She told me this a thousand times. She was never so tired at night that she didn't come in and pray with us. Our family went through a thousand crises, sometimes one a week, and the weight was always on my mom's shoulders. God gave her strength to survive and care for us.

"Ted, my younger brother, was always the black sheep of the family. Before he was even a teenager he used to get up in the middle of the night and go out and steal from people's garages. He and my older brother went to Vietnam. Teddy came back with a drug habit and my older brother, Tom, came back crippled. For the next twenty years they both lived at home with Mom. Teddy was arrested at least fifty times. At least fifty times my mom went through all the pain of courts, lawyers, bail bonds, visiting him in jail, and every single time she forgave him. He stole from everyone in the family, including my mom, and she always forgave him. She prayed and prayed he would someday turn to God. Everybody gave up on him except my mom. He was the outcast of the family. Two years ago he met a counselor in a rehab program who changed his life. The man finally convinced my brother to turn to God for help. Over the next six months Teddy's life slowly changed. Then he found this incredible woman, got married, and got a job in construction. In some ways he became the most God-filled man I ever knew. He lives for everybody but himself. Everyone was amazed but my mom. God helped her see the goodness in my brother when no one else could.

"She died about six weeks ago from cancer. It's strange to say but the last weeks of her life were the happiest. For about two weeks, my mom lay in bed and everyone who had ever known her came to visit. Through her love and generosity she had touched hundreds. I can see her right now in her deathbed, smiling, laughing even. I'll never forget when my father came to her, and they both were crying. She still loved him. I could see God in her face. She was dying and I could see God shining out of her face. Everyone was crying but she was happy."

Here is Ted's story.

"For as long as I can remember I've been wild. I always had too much energy. Nothing could hold me down. When I was nine and ten I used to go on forty-mile bike rides with a buddy of mine or we would jump on freight cars and ride them way out into the desert just to see where they went. I used to set the neighborhood cats on fire. I got involved in sports but I was never good enough, I was afraid my dad would see I was no good, so I'd quit and say I really wasn't interested. I used to break into people's houses and garages not to steal anything, but just to see the stuff they had. Maybe just take a spray can and paint the wall a little bit.

"When I got to be a teenager I had to have the hottest, fastest car. I had long hair. I was bad. I'd just ride around town feeling bad and looking for trouble. Finally the draft caught up to me and I went to Vietnam. I came back strung out on heroin. I can't count the number of houses I broke into. Hundreds. I stole everything from wedding rings to TV sets to washing machines. Anything I could sell to buy drugs. Every single time I went to jail I'd say this is the last time. I've finally learned my lesson. But the truth is that I was still angry inside, angry at God. I blamed everything on Him. I had this twisted idea that He didn't give me the life I wanted and so everything was His fault.

"Then I got into a counseling group in L.A. I met this guy

Paul. He was a big black guy, about six four, over two hundred fifty pounds. He'd been through everything I had. Vietnam, drugs, stealing, jail, everything. But he had found God. He kept after and after me. He challenged me to open my heart up and really pray. He made me see I was responsible for everything I'd done in my life. He made me see that I had brought so much pain into the world. I kept telling him to go to hell, get out of my face, but I could never tell him that he didn't understand what I'd been through. It was like we were brothers.

"Finally I just gave in and started praying with him. It was hard at first. I couldn't imagine that God would want anything to do with me. And I kept falling back into my old ways. But Paul stuck by my side and he taught me that his strength came from God. My life didn't change overnight. It wasn't that I was bad one evening and good the next morning. I'm still not living the way I want to. But I've learned how to turn to God and I've learned that He can give me strength. I lived a life of sin for forty years, and He never gave up on me. Man, is God patient!"

Now, as you think about these stories and the ways God touched your life in the past I want you to get ready for an important event. It's time for you to talk to God. Pour your heart out to Him. Tell Him about your past, about the ways He has guided you, about the people He brought into your life to help and guide you. Talk to Him about the best and worst of times. Tell Him about the times you felt His spirit and the times you felt far away from Him. Perhaps there are things that happened in your life that you don't understand. Talk to Him about these things. Perhaps you have done things you don't think could be forgiven. Tell Him and feel His forgiveness. Let Him help you begin a new life.

Talking to God about My Past

God, the first things I want to say to you are _____

_____

_____

_____

_____

_____

_____

_____.

And now I need to say _____

_____

_____

_____

_____

_____

_____

_____

_____

_____

_____

_____

_____

_____

_____

_____.

Look carefully at a normal day in your life now. You do and say and think certain things that take you closer to God. When you act from love or let yourself feel the love others have for you, then you are close to God. When you seek healing, when you try to help yourself and others to a better life, when you work toward your highest goals, when you dream the dreams that give you strength and joy, then you feel God's power. When you see all that is good in yourself and in others, then you see what God sees.

When you do things that destroy your strength and hope, when you hurt others, when you let yourself feel cut off from everyone, when you surrender to the darkness inside you and around you, when you don't care anymore what happens to you, then you have wandered far from God.

Everything that takes you farther from God is your old life. Everything that takes you closer to God is your new life.

I'll start by thinking about my old life. The thoughts that go through my head that take me away from God are _____

_____

_____

_____

_____

_____

_____.

The kinds of things I say to other people that take me away from God are _____

_____

_____

_____

_____.

The kinds of things I do that take me away from God are _____

_____

_____

_____

_____.

Now, I want to think about my new life. On a normal day, the kinds of things I think that take me closer to God are _____

_____

_____

_____

_____.

The kinds of things I say to other people that take me closer to God are _____

_____

_____.

The kinds of things I do that take me closer to God are _____

_____

_____

_____.

Listen to me. The easier it was for you to think of things related to your new life than to your old life, the more progress you are making. You are doing, saying, and thinking things that make the positive part of your life either stronger or weaker. Every minute of the day, you are helping yourself either to grow toward the Light or to stay in Darkness. Look at who you are right now. Describe your relationship to God.

When I think of my life now, the things in it that would please God are _____

_____

_____

_____
_____
_____
_____.

The things that would not please God are _____
_____
_____
_____.

There is one obvious reason you need a strong relationship with God. There is no way you can find a new life without Him. I have known thousands and thousands of teenagers who have over-come the most devastating problems humans can face. **But not one of them was victorious without finding God.** There is no way you can do it on your own. All the things you have learned in this book will help you. You certainly need all the insights you can get, you certainly need to see your relationships as clearly as possible, you certainly need to find at least one other person to rely on in the hard times ahead, but my forty years of experience have convinced me that you will never truly achieve your new life without God's help. Now, I am not saying you must read holy books every day. God will show you if that is the best way for you to be closer to Him. I am not even saying you must go to church or a synagogue. When you find God, He will teach you how you need to lead your new life. And I am certainly not saying that you need to be a Catholic or Baptist or even a Christian. The Jewish faith may speak powerfully to you or the Moslem faith. I believe there are many valid and powerful ways to live a spiritual life. But I can't emphasize this too strongly: **You have no chance without God.**

Look at your situation right now. There are powerful forces in society, probably in your family and friends, certainly in yourself that are driving you back into your old life. Look how long you have struggled and suffered. Look how helpless you have been to change without God. Look in your heart and you know the truth.

You have no chance of a new life, of realizing your dreams, of building a new personality without Him.

Dave, I believe _____

_____

_____

_____

_____

_____.

Now it's time for you to stop thinking about your new life and start living it.

The First Week of Your New Life

This is the last chapter of this book and I want you to begin your new life in the best possible way. The first thing we need to do is to sum up the progress you have made thus far. Look back at all you have said about yourself, others, your problems, and your relationship to God. What are the most basic lessons you have learned about who you are?

When I look back at what I have written in this book, I see I am someone who _____

_____

_____

_____.

When I look at my past, I see someone who was _____

_____

_____

_____

_____.

When I look at my present, I see someone who is _____

_____

_____

_____ .

If I do not escape from my old life, then what I see myself becoming in the future is _____

_____

_____ .

But if I continue forward with my new life, I see myself becoming in the future _____

_____

_____ .

Of everything I have learned about myself, the most important lesson is _____

_____

_____

_____ .

And what can you teach yourself right now about your relationships? Which relationships strengthen your new life, which weaken it?

My relationships with _____

_____

strengthen my new life, and my relationships with _____

_____

_____ could

destroy it. Therefore, what I need to do is _____
_____,
because _____
_____
_____.

The most important lesson I can teach myself about my relationships is _____
_____
_____.

And what have you learned about your spiritual life?

I can strengthen my relationship to God by _____
_____

and by _____
_____

and by _____
_____
_____.

Or I can weaken my relationship to God by _____
_____
_____

and by _____
_____

and by _____
_____.

The most important lesson I can teach myself about my spiritual life is _____

_____

_____.

    I want you to see that you are at a very important moment right now. Picking up this book and working through it was a major step forward. But you are like a toddler, you are just beginning your new life. You have taken a few steps forward, but you are weak. You must be extremely careful not to give in to temptation. If you fall back into your old life you could lose everything. If you have been seriously involved with drugs and you take one hit on a joint or pop one pill, or if you have been seriously involved with alcohol and you take one swallow of beer, wine, or hard liquor, then **you are risking everything.** Do you understand what I'm telling you? You have to stay completely away from situations and people that lead you back to your old life.

    Dave, I see that _____

_____

_____.

    You see your old life clearly now. You see what it has done to you and the people you love. You know exactly what you do that makes your old life stronger. You know what destroys you. But the temptations are tremendously strong. The habits that led you into Darkness are still alive. This is why I have one piece of advice to guide you through the week ahead. You must do everything in your power to cling to God.

    Therefore, you have only one goal. Do as much as you can each day for the next week that will make you feel close to God. Do as little as possible that will make you feel far from Him. It won't be easy. You will have temptations to return to your old life on the first day. Here is a list of suggestions of things to do which will strengthen your new life and, therefore, your relationship with God. Some will not apply, others might seem corny, but some will leap off the page and speak directly to you. Put a check mark by those.

    To start living a new life I can:

1. Take no more drugs.
2. Drink no more alcohol.
3. Stay away from people who are an important part of my old life.
4. Spend more time with people who are an important part of my new life.
5. Find someone to talk to about my problems.
6. Work on one relationship to make it stronger.
7. Start an exercise program.
8. Eat foods that are better for me.
9. Stop smoking.
10. Change the kind of music I listen to.
11. Find something new to do when I am bored.
12. Go to church.
13. Read the Bible.
14. Talk to someone about my spiritual life.
15. Help someone I love.
16. Help someone find a new life.
17. Surprise someone with an act of love.
18. Help someone work through a copy of this book.
19. Join an alcohol or drug rehabilitation group.
20. Record my thoughts and feelings in a journal.
21. Stop watching so much TV.
22. Pray.
23. Show love to a pet.
24. Give myself praise.
25. Tell someone how much I love them.
26. Bring a small group of friends together and talk about how we can help each other lead new lives.
27. Do something I've always dreamed of doing.
28. Get more involved in an art activity I enjoy.
29. Set a goal that I can make progress toward day by day.
30. Start a new relationship with a brother or sister.
31. Do something at home that will help the family.
32. Spend more time listening.
33. Spend more time opening up.
34. Get a physical and start solving my health problems.
35. Take a long walk every day.
36. Get involved in a sport I really enjoy.
37. Visit someone who is lonely.
38. Make plans for the greatest summer I've ever had.
39. Save money for something I really want.
40. Amaze one of my parents by spending more time with him or her.
41. Don't go anywhere on the weekends.
42. Get out of the house on weekends.
43. Join a church group.
44. Teach someone how to do something.
45. Write Dave a letter! (My address is at the end of this chapter.)
46. Smile more.
47. Change how I dress.
48. Look people in the eye.
49. Tell everyone who needs to know that I've started a new life.
50. Make something beautiful.

Look back at the suggestions you've checked. Pick only a few, maybe even only one, that you can work on this week. Then plan your new life. Keep the plan simple and clear. Remember, you are either moving forward toward your new life or you are standing still in your old life. For example, if you said you need to quit smoking then each day you don't smoke is part of your new life and each day you do smoke is part of your old life. Keep moving forward!

The specific things I'm going to do this week to continue my new life are _____

_____

_____

_____.

Each day I will know I am moving forward if _____

_____

_____

_____.

And I will know I am making no progress if _____

_____

_____

_____.

The rest of this chapter is a seven-day journal. At the end of each day, make at least three entries. First, describe how your plan for a new life worked on that day; second, sum up whether you are moving forward or standing still; and third, give yourself advice for the next day.

The First Day of My New Life

What happened today was _____

_____
_____
_____
_____
_____
_____
_____
_____
_____
_____
_____
_____
_____.

When I think about whether I am standing still or moving forward, I see _____

_____
_____
_____
_____.

The advice I have for myself about tomorrow is _____

_____
_____.

The Second Day of My New Life

What happened today was _____
_____
_____
_____
_____
_____
_____
_____
_____
_____.

When I think about whether I am standing still or moving forward, I see _____
_____
_____
_____.

The advice I have for myself about tomorrow is _____
_____
_____.

The Third Day of My New Life

What happened today was _____

_____

_____

_____

_____

_____

_____

_____

_____

_____

_____

_____

_____

_____.

When I think about whether I am standing still or moving forward, I see _____

_____

_____

_____

_____.

The advice I have for myself about tomorrow is _____

_____

_____.

The Fourth Day of My New Life

What happened today was _____

_____

_____

_____

_____

_____

_____

_____

_____

_____

_____

_____

_____.

When I think about whether I am standing still or moving
forward, I see _____

_____

_____

_____.

The advice I have for myself about tomorrow is _____

_____

_____.

The Fifth Day of My New Life

What happened today was _____

_____

_____

_____

_____

_____

_____

_____

_____

_____

_____

_____

_____.

When I think about whether I am standing still or moving
forward, I see _____

_____

_____

_____.

The advice I have for myself about tomorrow is _____

_____

_____.

The Sixth Day of My New Life

What happened today was _____

_____

_____

_____

_____

_____

_____

_____

_____

_____

_____

_____

_____

_____ .

When I think about whether I am standing still or moving forward, I see _____

_____

_____

_____

_____ .

The advice I have for myself about tomorrow is _____

_____

_____ .

The Seventh Day of My New Life

What happened today was _____

_____

_____

_____

_____

_____

_____

_____

_____

_____

_____

_____

_____

_____.

When I think about whether I am standing still or moving forward, I see _____

_____

_____

_____

_____.

The advice I have for myself about tomorrow is _____

_____

_____.

Congratulations! You have accomplished something truly amazing. Look back through this book at all the wisdom you have found inside yourself. You have taught yourself what you needed to know about so many areas of your life! And even better, you just finished a week in which you put your ideas into practice. What you have achieved is one of your life's great victories. With your own strength and will and courage, you have turned your life around and beaten all the dark forces that were holding you back. There is no stopping you now. You have found health and strength inside you and you have the wisdom you need to seek a great and beautiful future.

You are wonderful. Please feel my love for you. Right now as I write these words I am hoping with all my heart that you can feel how proud I am of what you have accomplished. You are a wonder and a miracle and I thank God that He brought us together.

Please let me hear from you!

Write to

David Toma
P.O. Box 854
Clark, NJ 07066

For more information about my video, "Toma—Live on Stage," in the United States call 1-800-966-3339; in Canada call 1-800-533-9239.

Appendix
People and Organizations
That Can Help You

Al-Anon Family Groups, P.O. Box 862, Midtown Station, New York,
   NY 10018.
These groups are for the families of alcoholics. You can request a
listing for Al-Anon, Alateen, and ACOA (Adult Children of Alcoholics) meetings by calling 1-800-344-2666.

Alcoholics Anonymous (AA).
There are AA groups in practically every town and city in the
United States. They hold meetings 365 days a year, at all hours
of the day. Check your local telephone listings for the group nearest you.

Alliance for Recovery (ARI), 36 Newark Avenue, Belleville, NJ 07109;
   national hotline, 1-800-238-1705.
ARI is a *free* and confidential referral service able to place you in
twelve-step inpatient recovery/rehabilitation programs nationwide
for drug and substance abuse; eating disorders, including anorexia
and bulimia; adult children of alcoholics; and codependency. If you
think, or have been told, that you might have any of these problems, please contact ARI immediately. The centers it recommends
accept most major medical insurance.

Cult Awareness Network, 2421 West Pratt Avenue, Suite 1173,
  Chicago, IL 60645; 312-267-7777.
This national organization with forty-five affiliates was founded in
1979 and provides public information and education about satanic
and destructive mind-control cults. It also provides support and
assistance for friends and families of cult members, and help for
former cult members.

Domestic Violence Hotline, P.O. Box 7070, Trenton, NJ 08628;
  1-800-572-SAFE.
Call to receive information, crisis intervention, and referrals.

Gamblers Anonymous, 1315 West State Street, Trenton, NJ 08618;
  1-800-426-2537.
Call or write to receive meeting information for Gamblers Anonymous and Gama-Teen meetings nationwide.

Looking Up, P.O. Box K, Augusta, ME 04332-0470; 207-626-3402.
This organization serves survivors of child sexual abuse and incest.
It offers support and counseling via mail or telephone, and work-
shops and retreats are available. Ask about its publications—the
"Looking Up" Times, and the *Survivor Resource Chronicle.*

National AIDS Hotline, 1-800-342-2437.

National Association for Children of Alcoholics (NACOA), 31582 Coast
  Highway #B, South Laguna, CA 92677.
NACOA provides literature, national referrals, and networking for
children of alcoholics of all ages. Send a self-addressed, stamped
envelope for more information or referrals.

National Association of Anorexia Nervosa and Associated Disorders Inc.,
  P.O. Box 7, Highland Park, IL 60035; 312-831-3438.
This international organization with more than 200 affiliated groups
provides information on self-help groups, therapy, and referrals.

National Center for Missing and Exploited Children, 2102 Wilson Blvd.
  #550, Arlington, VA 22201; 703-235-3900; national hotline,
  1-800-843-5678.
The center serves as a clearinghouse for missing children.

National Institute of Drug Abuse Hotline, 1-800-662-HELP.
This national information line offers referrals to treatment programs, twelve-step meetings, and state-funded programs.

National Survivors of Child Abuse Program (NCAP), P.O. Box 630,
Hollywood, CA 90028; national hotline, 1-800-422-4453.
NCAP provides networking, advocacy, resources, and public education on abuse-related issues. It also offers guided twelve-step programs. Call its National Abuse Hotline if you are in crisis, or you would like to report child abuse.

Parents Anonymous, 6733 South Sepulveda Blvd., Los Angeles, CA
90045; national hotline 1-800-421-0353.
Parents Anonymous is a crisis intervention program to help parents who have abused their children, or are afraid they might. Its national hotline provides referrals and information. Other services (such as free support groups) vary from state to state.

Planned Parenthood Federation of America.
Planned Parenthood consists of 172 affiliates with more than 800 clinics nationwide. They provide reproductive health services for women and male and female adolescents, including gynecological care, examinations and treatment for sexually transmitted diseases, as well as birth control counseling. Check your telephone directory for the center nearest you. Although each affiliate operates differently, most use a sliding pay scale, so you pay only what you can afford.

Suicide Prevention Hotline, 249 East Ocean Blvd., Suite 888, Long
Beach, CA 90802; 1-800-882-3386.
This twenty-four-hour hotline provides crisis support and referral information for depression and alcohol and substance abuse to local community mental health programs.

Youth Crisis Hotline (Runaway Hotline), P.O. Box 178408, San Diego,
CA 92177-8408; 1-800-448-4663.
Call to receive information, support, and referrals to counselors and centers nationwide.

About the Authors

David Toma is a legend in his own time. For the last forty years he has been America's leading antidrug and antialcohol crusader, speaking to thousands of teenagers, parents, teachers, and school administrators each week. The inspiration for two television series —"Baretta" and "Toma"—he was a policeman for twenty-one years and is also a former Marine drill instructor. For sixteen of his years on the force he was a detective in the vice, gambling, and narcotics squad of one of North America's most troubled cities, Newark, New Jersey. His arrest record was unmatched—numbering in the thousands with an unheard-of 98 percent conviction record—all without ever firing his gun. He has lectured throughout the world, is the author of four books including *Toma Tells It Straight—With Love*, and has hosted his own weekly discussion program on New York's WOR-TV. He lives with his family in Clark, New Jersey.

Christopher Biffle has taught philosophy for twenty years. He has received the American Academy of Poets Prize and grants from both the National Endowment for the Humanities and the U.S. Department of Education. He is the author of seven books, including *The Castle of the Pearl* and *A Journey Through Your Childhood*, which feature his unique interactive approach to problem solving. He is the father of two daughters, and he and his family live in southern California.